Used

To be

UU

The Systematic Attack

On UU Liberalism

What You Need to Know

What You Need to Do

Frank Casper
Jay Kiskel

This book was published by the Fifth Principle Project. The Fifth Principle Project is a grassroots initiative to gather into community Unitarian Universalists who want to reinvigorate the right of conscience and renew the democratic process in the governing of our denomination. This grassroots movement was initiated on January 4, 2020 when a letter was sent to more than 1,000 congregations to bring to light a concern that our denominational UU leadership had lost touch with the spirit of its mission to serve the member congregations of the Association and was no longer listening to the voices of everyday UUs. This loss of connection with congregations and UUs has been accompanied by a continuing embrace by our UU leadership of a top down, ideologically driven governing model. Such a governing model overturns norms that have long been part of the governance of the denomination and threatens the democratic foundations of UUism. Only by exercising our collective voting power can we have a voice in setting the direction of our faith movement.

Learn more about the Fifth Principle Project at FifthPrincipleProject.org. Visit our homepage and join the Fifth Principle Project for free. You will then be able to stay involved in this effort to defend UUism.

Acknowledgments

We wish to thank Helen Borland, Cate Duggar, and Jim Aiken for their editing services. Cate and Jim, professional writers and concerned Unitarian Universalists, are also thanked for their guidance on narrative structure. We also want to recognize others who contributed chapters to the Governance section of this book; Rev. Rick Davis, Rev. Richard Trudeau, Rev. Cate Rohde, and a minister who wished to remain anonymous out of concern for professional consequences. We also want to recognize the valuable feedback we received from our team of readers who reviewed the pre-publication manuscript and offered their comments.

About the Authors

Frank Casper has been a member of the Unitarian Universalist Congregation of Atlanta since 1993. He has served in several positions over time, including head of Adult Religious Education. He has preached throughout the Mid-South District. He is currently lay minister emeritus after ten years as a lay minister of UUCA.

Jay Kiskel has been a member of the Northwest Unitarian Universalist Congregation since 1988. He has served on his congregation's board as well as on the Mid-South District board and the board of The Mountain, a UU-identified camp and retreat center in North Carolina. He is currently the president of the Universalist Convocation, which sponsors annual meetings so Universalists can gather and celebrate our Universalist heritage.

Disclaimer

While the authors of this book appeal to all Unitarian Universalists, we speak only for ourselves on behalf of The Fifth Principle Project. We do not speak for our respective congregations.

Table of Contents

Table of Contents

Introduction

We assume you are reading this book either because you are intrigued by the main title, or because you are concerned by the subtitle, "The Systematic Attack on UU Liberalism. What You Need to Know. What You Need to Do." Either way, we, the authors, are hoping you will read this book so we may share with you our understanding of disturbing trends within Unitarian Universalism that may substantively alter UUism. To set a baseline, Unitarian Universalism is the inheritor of values from our heritage denominations. We value self-expression, reason, logic, science, and critical thinking from the first U in our combined denomination. We value compassion and love from the second U. Mostly we have the freedom to pursue our own path, to search or not search. It is not that UUs are rudderless, characterized as some pejoratively suggest by "believing in anything we want." Our Seven Principles are an expression of our communal aspirations. We are not required to believe in the inherent worth and dignity of every person. We just do. Such is the case with our other principles.

Our principles' strength is that they did not just appear when Unitarians and Universalists agreed to merge in 1961. Liberal values such as individual dignity, justice, equity, religious tolerance, democracy, and personal liberty emerged in the 17th and 18th centuries in a period called the Age of Enlightenment. That period ushered in the modern era, in which we have left behind the dominion of clerics and monarchs, the sway of religion over science, and the subjugation of individual liberty. We have come to accept the norms of the modern age as enlightened. Unfortunately, change to those norms is occurring in UUism.

The changes to UUism have not been hidden but have been invisible to most UUs. That invisibility is due to our natural focus on our congregations. For most UUs, decisions at the Unitarian Universalist Association (UUA) level in Boston are distant noise easily tuned out. In many ways, our inattention has contributed to the concerns we wish to raise, the acceptance by UU leadership of ideological theories antithetical to UU liberalism and the atrophy of democracy in denomination governance.

Nearly a decade ago changes to the Association's bylaws weakened the role of democracy in the denomination. Those changes consolidated our nineteen districts into five regions and eliminated the representation of local UUs on the board in favor of at-large members. Can you name, for instance, one currently serving UUA Board of Trustees member? Another significant change was the creation of a central Nominating Committee, as opposed to the decentralized district method, to identify candidates for the UUA Board of Trustees. This centralized Nominating Committee has among its objectives to bring diversity with regard to race, gender, and sexual orientation or identity to the composition of the board. The Nominating Committee may have achieved its objective of diversity, but, in our opinion, has failed to achieve diversity of thought and now is essentially a gatekeeper to preserve the ideological mindset of the board. Diversity of thought drives rigorous debate ensuring that board decisions are carefully considered. Such debate should inform any board decision since the UUA Board has wide-ranging explicit and implicit powers. Unchecked by competing points of view or constituent voices, the board is unfettered in its decision-making. Consider the 2017 declaration by the UUA Board of Trustees that UUism is based on white supremacy and is racist and oppressive. That decision, rendered in 90 minutes by only a handful of people, clearly was not subjected to critical debate or considerations regarding the ramifications such a decision would have on UUism. That decision charging UUism with harboring white supremacy has set into motion activities that could very well result in inappropriate changes to our principles and upend our congregational autonomy.

We tend not to recognize the real implications of UU leadership decisions because they are typically articulated in the cloak of a social justice endeavor, such as a drive for diversity. You may have heard the outlines of this social justice endeavor expressed in terms such as beloved community and accountable relationships. Few, if any UUs, would disagree with the goal of diversity. Poorly understood, however, is the darker reality that beneath this call for diversity are external ideologies antithetical to UU liberal values that have been woven into the fabric of UU leadership thinking. We will provide more information about these ideologies in this book. For now, it is important only to understand that these ideologies have a very well-defined prescription on how to cleanse the denomination of its alleged white supremacy. The cleansing involves an uprooting of our UU liberal values and a concerted effort to revise our principles.

It is not alarmist to believe, as we do at the Fifth Principle Project, that UUism is under attack. The authors of this book are involved UUs. We have done extensive research, have consulted with others, and have subjected our conclusions to critical debate. We now wish to share our findings. After reading this book we ask that you come to your own conclusion about the threat to UUism. In the end, it may be that a majority of Unitarian Universalists concur that UUism is based on white supremacy and choose to accept limited democracy. However, there is no way to know what degree of consensus there is unless the stresses now being placed on UUism are widely known and debated. Having a denomination-wide conversation is difficult since the UUA Board controls all channels for mass communication, the Association's budget, and sets the agenda for General Assembly. We have no way of communicating with UUs across the nation. Therefore, we wrote this book as a vehicle for UUs to begin, at a minimum, one-on-one conversations. If you are concerned after reading this book, then we urge you to make your concerns known to your fellow congregants and your congregation's leadership. Express your congregation's concern to our UU leadership. Become a delegate at General Assembly and knowledgeably vote on changes proposed to our principles and sources. We want any decisions made to be based on our Fifth Principle, the democratic principle that fosters diversity, of race and gender for sure, but also of thought and individual expression.

When our UU values are threatened, every UU should be engaged.

Frank Casper
Jay Kiskel
Founders of the Fifth Principle Project
March 2021

History

1.   White Supremacy: How the Decision Was Made

On April 3, 2017, just two days after Rev. Peter Morales resigned two and a half months before completing his second four-year term as president of the UUA, the UUA Board of Trustees held its first board meeting via Zoom. One can only imagine the immense weight of responsibility the board felt to address the succession process to fill the vacant presidency and to calm the anger and recriminations that surrounded the departure of Rev. Morales.

Just a month earlier, Rev. Scott Tayler, the Director of Congregational Life, had hired Rev. Andy Burnette, the senior minister from Valley Unitarian Universalist Congregation in Chandler, Arizona, to replace Rev. Ken Hurto, who was retiring as the Southern Region Director. The hiring of Burnette, a white male, resulted in a swift and public outcry from UU religious professionals of color, who had gathered on March 17 for their annual Finding Our Way Home retreat.[1] One of the religious professionals present at the retreat was Christina Rivera, the Director of Administration and Finance at Thomas Jefferson Memorial Church UU in Charlottesville, Virginia. Rivera, a Chicana Latina, was, like Burnette, a member of the UUA Board of Trustees and

7

an applicant for the Southern Region Director position. Rivera told colleagues that she had been a finalist for the position but had been told that she was not "the right fit for the team."[2] Over the next few weeks, charges spread over social media that another white person had been hired over what was reported in *UUA World* as a "woman of color who was a qualified finalist."[3] In May, shortly after his resignation, Rev. Morales broke his silence in a lengthy Facebook post that undercut the prevailing narrative fueling the controversy. "The narrative is that she [Christina Rivera] was not hired because she is a Latina. Let me be as clear as I can be: this is simply false. . . The uncritical acceptance of a false narrative and the assumption of the moral inferiority of leaders led naturally to what looks more like an inquisition than like the Beloved Community."[4] Charges and counter-charges filled social media with rancor. It was a time, in retrospect, we could all agree did not well represent our UU values.

White Supremacy Declaration

Such was the environment that the Board of Trustees faced as they settled into their 8:00 PM Zoom meeting. The meeting began with a deep-dive check-in, from which observers were barred. The board then entered into a 30-minute executive session to "consider personnel issues." The meeting adjourned at 9:30 PM and produced two outputs.

One output was the UUA Interim Presidency Transition Plan. This plan assumedly would encompass the objectives, responsibilities, and timeline for filling the presidential vacancy until the next election

8

at General Assembly on June 24, 2017. However, except for step five of the plan, which read, "Ensure an adequate transition plan is in place for the incoming president," the transition plan was a public attack on the culture of UUism. UU culture was declared to harbor "structures and patterns that foster racism, oppression, and white supremacy." This axiomatic assertion was offered as an assumed self-evident truth that was beyond challenge. The board operationalized this declaration with a formal call to establish a process to analyze structural racism and white supremacy within the UUA.[5] This action resulted in the creation of the Commission on Institutional Change (COIC), which delivered its final report, entitled *Widening the Circle of Concern,* at the 2020 virtual General Assembly.

The second output produced was an action to sponsor UU White Supremacy Teach-Ins at member congregations and communities. The focus of the teach-ins was to "discuss the realities of racism and white supremacy in our congregations, in our Association, and in our faith." People were instructed to sign up for the teach-ins at the Black Lives UU (BLUU) website.[6]

In the wake of the declaration that our denomination fostered racism, oppression, and white supremacy, two questions arise. First, just how did a failed hiring effort result in a sweeping white supremacy indictment? All organizations, from churches and non-profits to small businesses and large corporations sometimes see controversy arise over a hiring decision. Few if any of them change their entire culture and purpose. The second question is, did the board have the authority to thrust the denomination into a divisive cycle of accusation and recrimination that some argue threatens the very foundation of liberalism upon which UUism rests?

Answers to Questions

The answer to the first question, how did a failed hiring result in such tumult, is complicated and takes us into what some regard as the obscure ideological territory of applied postmodernism and ideas it spawned, such as Critical Race Theory. We will address postmodernism and critical theories in Chapter 7, "New UU Orthodoxy." We want to stress that the reader doesn't need to be an expert in applied postmodernism and critical theories. What is important to understand is how these ideologies have supplanted UU liberal values in the decision-making process by our UU leadership. Without this insight, none of the board's April 2017 actions or the recommendations by the Commission on Institutional Change will make any sense.

To the second question, did the Board of Trustees have the authority to make such a sweeping declaration regarding the character of our denomination? The unfortunate answer is yes. Given the short duration of the meeting, it does not appear that the allegation that UUism harbored white supremacy was "discovered" during the 90-minute meeting. It is much more likely that this ideological belief entered the room with the board members. Holding such a view meant that there was no need for open deliberation, reflective consideration, or solicited counsel. The decision effectively bypassed the Association's democratic safeguards and removed everyday UUs from the decision. This unilateral decision raises a question yet to be answered: Just how on earth did such an important decision impacting the entire denomination get made without democratic debate? Are the trustees of the UUA Board not responsive to the voices of UUs across the nation?

Broken Democracy

Democracy is fundamental to the governance of our congregations and denomination. We hold congregational meetings to elect our board members, call a minister, or approve a budget. No big decision is taken without open discussion and then a vote. Democracy only works when there is an understanding that ultimate authority resides in the members of the congregation.

We extend this concept of "power to the people" to representative democracy when we elect board and committee members. Representative democracy works because we extend trust to our elected members that they will act in the interests of the congregation and the members. Trust, however, is neither absolute nor free of inspection. As a Sufi saying puts it, "Trust in God, but tie down your camel." Our congregation-elected board and committee members must renew their compact of trust by continually listening to the voices of their fellow congregants.

At the national denominational level, governance is similar but different. As in our congregations, at the national level, there is a Board of Trustees that governs the denomination between our annual General Assemblies. The board is composed of the president (without vote), eleven trustees, two youth trustees, a financial advisor, and a moderator. The direct and discretionary authority we have entrusted in the board is sweeping. The board, for example, defines the rules for the admission of congregations to the Association, determines how our Annual Program Fund (APF) dues from our congregations are spent, makes the rules for the accreditation of delegates and voting procedures at General Assembly, and sets the agenda for the General Assembly.

Unlike the members of our congregational board of trustees, our national trustees are not compelled to listen to the voices of UUs in our congregations. By design, there is no direct representation of UUs at the national level. All the UUA trustees are at-large members and thus not accountable to any regional or local constituents. Some might find assurance that at least the annual General Assembly is a firewall against any overreach of board actions. Indeed, General Assembly can be a check on board overreach, but it is not structurally configured to provide such oversight.

The annual General Assembly gathers thousands of UUs and voting delegates from congregations across the nation, allowing individual UUs to participate directly in the business of the Association. Delegates cast votes for president, bylaws changes, and other business requiring direct consent by congregational delegates. However, as early as October 2007, the shortcomings of General Assembly to conduct the business of the denomination were recognized. As a result, the Fifth Principle Task Force was commissioned by the UUA Board to provide recommendations to align General Assembly as a truly representative delegate body. The Task Force released its final report in December 2009 and succinctly observed that General Assembly as a governing body was "dramatically broken."

The reality is that for the vast majority of UUs, their orbit of engagement is centered around their congregations. It may be said that most UUs are only loosely engaged with matters regarding the UUA in Boston, though it may be more accurate to observe that most UUs know little of national denominational politics and have little incentive to increase their knowledge. We see this engagement level in our congregations, where only a handful of people repeatedly attend General Assembly and others never show any interest. At General Assembly, delegates generally vote to pass motions with overwhelming majorities. Absent any personal interest or any interest invested in a delegate by a congregation; this mass voting reflects a natural desire to trust our leadership and support their endeavors. It is also difficult to be a minority voter in a social setting. This inclination to trust our leadership and vote without questioning is the undoing of our Fifth Principle and, by extension, undermines UUism. For the health of the denomination, General Assembly delegates, and UUs in general, must cease being passive and become active policymakers.

Why Do I Care?

I admit (co-author Jay) that I was like many other UUs and was only vaguely aware of what was going on at the national level in Boston. My focus was on my congregation. In 2017 that disinterest changed when I took a keen interest in who would be the new Southern Region Director.

I live in the Southern Region of the Atlanta area. In my retirement, I became a historian keen to gather, archive, and write about southern Universalist history. I signed up for the 2017 New Orleans General Assembly with the expectation of meeting the new Southern Region Director and securing the new director's sponsorship for my southern historical work. When the hiring effort for that position exploded into recriminations and eventually a white supremacy declaration, I was completely bewildered. I was equally bewildered at the 2017 General Assembly by the frequent mention of how UUism needed to be liberated from its white supremacy. How had a faith tradition that had held my fidelity for thirty-plus years so suddenly collapse into such rancor?

To find an answer, I redirected my research skills to study events leading up to the April 2017 white supremacy controversy. To be sure, I fell down many rabbit holes trying to understand what was going on. I eventually learned that the white supremacy decision was made by only a handful of people whose actions exhibited an ideological inclination. The reason that a small group of people was able to have such a significant impact on UUism is that our UU leadership has become more influenced by advocacy groups and less responsive to the UUs who fill the seats in our congregations. Although the shell of democratic governance is still standing, much of the Association's governance is now unrepresentative. Absent a functioning representative democracy, small groups of people who have access to the resources of the Association can pursue their agendas unimpeded by oversight or the clamor of dissenting voices.

What is the Prize?

We at the Fifth Principle Project can now see that an ideological influence operating in an organization whose democratic norms have atrophied can enable a few people to make a sweeping declaration that the denomination is based on white supremacy culture and is therefore racist. Less clear is the specific objective or prize sought by this declaration. If the objective includes the elimination of racism, no Unitarian Universalists, including the authors and contributors to this book, would deny that all UUs are committed to dismantling racism wherever it continues to exist! This commitment to confronting racism is baked into our Seven Principles, our history of being on the front lines of the civil rights movement, and our ever-renewing efforts to expand human rights.

It is appropriate to ask if this declaration of the denomination's complicity with white supremacy is a continuation of our historic commitment to justice, equity, and compassion or something different.

This book argues that the charge of white supremacy is something different. Rather than centering our Seven Principles in the battle for equality in some innovative way, the charge of white supremacy has turned the core of the denomination's liberal values upside down. The charge of racism has now been weaponized against our liberal values and our religious heritages. UUism, in this new era of ubiquitous perceptions of white supremacy culture, is no longer seen as a cure but as a source of white supremacy.

That last statement is difficult to comprehend. We ask that you keep an open mind while reading this book. Many UUs would unflinchingly commit to centering our UU liberal values in a new 21st century UU civil rights movement focused on the elimination of racism. It cannot, however, be denied that there are official actions sponsored by our UU leadership that question the value of our liberal values and our Seven Principles.

Pay Attention Here

You are encouraged to carefully follow two ongoing UUA Board-sponsored initiatives. The first is the UUA Board's effort to implement the recommendations of the Commission on Institutional Change, as contained in its report *Widening the Circle of Concern*. There is, for example, a very clear implication that our Fourth Principle, a free and responsible search for truth and meaning, is to be restricted by a vaguely defined accountability known as "boundaries of community." See Chapter 8, "The Demolition of the Fourth Principle" for more information. Changes to the Fourth Principle and other COIC recommendations will require votes at General Assembly.

The second initiative is the Article II Study Commission, which was established in 2020 and charged to review the section of the bylaws containing our principles, sources, the purpose of the Association, inclusion objectives, and freedom of belief statement. Although the commission was to present its draft recommendations at the January 2021 board meeting, this did not occur. Rather the Article II Study Commission (A2SC) shared with the board its progress regarding the creation of educational materials and a history of our UU principles and sources. See Chapter 5, "Article II Study Commission: Story of our Principles" for an overview of the history of our principles. The A2SC indicated that it was planning a virtual "Collaboratory" style event in the spring of 2021 where "stakeholders can have conversations together."[7] The Fifth Principle Project has requested to be an official stakeholder and included in conversations with other stakeholders.

Despite the small setback in the delivery of initial draft changes, it appears the high-level calendar of events for the Article II Study Commission remains unimpacted. That is, recommendations for changes to Article II will be presented for a first vote at the 2022 General Assembly. If those Article II recommendations are accepted, a final vote is scheduled to take place at the 2023 General Assembly.

The most appropriate action you can take as a concerned UU is to use the power of the Fifth Principle and the power of your vote.

Consider running by petition to become a trustee of the UUA Board. Become a delegate at General Assembly in 2021, 2022, and 2023. Read all proposals, reflect on their impact on UUism, and then vote wisely. Be informed. Be active. Move from loosely connected to fully engaged. The fate of UUism rests on your vote.

2.   Fifth Principle Task Force

"We should get serious about governing
ourselves democratically or I will move in 2010 that
we rescind the Fifth Principle until we can prove we
are democratically represented."[8]

Denise Davidoff, former UUA moderator and chairperson of the Fifth Principle Task Force, threw down that challenge at the 2009 Salt Lake City General Assembly.[9] Her challenge came nearly two years after the Task Force began its work in October 2007 to determine how General Assembly could be more accessible, representative, inclusive, and democratic. Sadly, during the six-year discussion on the Task Force's recommendations, the governance of the UUA progressively drifted away from the spirit of our Fifth Principle. Over that time, the board lost its focus on its mandate "to serve the needs of its member congregations."[10] Instead, the board turned inward and became consumed with internal debates on its governance model, diversity, covenanting, and accountability.

Having read more than ten years of board meeting minutes, reports, General Assembly presentations, and *UU World* articles researching the Fifth Principle Task Force's history, I (co-author Jay) came to recognize the board's gradual abandonment of its servant leadership role. The board slowly, but consistently, assumed a self-appointed posture that it was the ultimate governing authority within the denomination.

We arrived here because there were years of missed opportunities to engage the governing energy of the denomination. When the interim Fifth Principle Task Force Report was introduced in the Spring of 2009, there was considerable enthusiasm. The subtitle of the report, "Reformulation of General Assembly: Status Quo is Not an Option," harkened back to the sense of resolve of "Failure is not an option" in the rescue of the Apollo 13 mission when the service module suffered catastrophic damage on its lunar voyage. The Task Force members were genuinely dedicated to achieving a transformational change in General Assembly. They sought to make the annual assembly economically accessible and sustainable. They wanted knowledgeable delegates authorized to represent congregations with well-understood accountability between the Association and congregations.[11]

Why General Assembly is Broken

The Fifth Principle Task Force completed its report in December 2009. The report made clear that the UUA Board of Trustees was not the denomination's ultimate decision-making authority but that the board was accountable to congregational delegates at General Assembly. "A central principle of policy-style governance is a board's assurance that it acts as the informed voice of the organization's sources of authority and accountability—its moral owners." The report continued, "The primary sources of authority and accountability for our UUA Board of Trustees are the duly elected and called leaders of the member congregations, and specifically member congregations' delegates to the UUA General Assembly."[12]

The report observed the structural deficiencies of General Assembly:

- General Assembly is not really democratic in that delegates are neither representative of their congregations, other than being members, nor are they accountable to their congregation;
- Without subsidization of delegates, General Assembly is economically discriminatory, and therefore generationally discriminatory;
- As long as General Assembly continues as an annual event, its cost is a heavy burden to the Association and the member congregations;
- The General Assembly process is not in alignment with the board's embrace of policy governance.

Although the Board of Trustees is accountable to the "congregational delegates" at General Assembly, the assembled delegates are not representative of the Association's congregations. Fewer than 60% of member congregations have one or more delegates at General Assembly, meaning that 40% of the Association's congregations are not represented. Many delegates self-select and self-fund their attendance. There is no formal mechanism to educate attending delegates on the business to be decided at General Assembly. Most significantly, the very nature of General Assembly to be a body of "congregational delegates" is undermined when little or no guidance on how to vote on issues is given to delegates by their home congregation. This situation renders delegates just individuals voting their personal preferences with no accountability back to their home congregation. Thus, the Fifth Principle Task Force concluded that General Assembly was "dramatically broken."

Among the Task Force's recommendations was to conduct biennial delegate assemblies in odd years where the business of the Association could be decided by a smaller number of knowledgeable delegates whose cost would be subsidized. The Task Force was quite explicit that attendance at these delegate assemblies was for congregational delegates, the UUA Board and administration. There would be no delegates from associate member organizations such as the UU Service Committee and UU Women's Federation, nor would there be any UUA Board of Trustee delegates. This attendance recommendation emphasized that the Unitarian Universalist Association was composed of autonomous, self-governing congregations that voluntarily chose to unite together. The design envisioned for the delegate assemblies was such that member congregations could focus on the governance of their Association. There was an expectation that congregational delegates were to be elected and certified by their congregation to be accountable not only to their congregation but also to neighboring delegate teams. To enable geographic or community-based governance, the Task Force recommended that seating at the General Assembly plenary sessions should be geographically arranged with intentional space designated on the assembly floor for cross-communication and cooperation. The Task Force offered this expectation, "Know our neighbors to build UU community & effectiveness beyond the walls of our congregations."[13]

It was further recommended that in even years a program-rich General Assembly should be held. The program-rich assemblies could be organized as "Big Tent" assemblies similar to the current General Assembly structure. Alternatively, assemblies could be thematically aligned regional gatherings or simply a Unitarian Universalist "Week of Service."[14]

To underscore the need for reform, the Task Force offered a stern warning, "The future of our UU movement can ill-afford to continue the ways of faux democracy and unaccountable representation that have characterized Associational governance, including the content and process of General Assembly."[15]

Despite the peril posed by our institutionally sanctioned faux democracy, none of the key recommendations of the Fifth Principle Task Force were adopted. Once a headline conversation at General Assembly, by the 2015 Portland General Assembly, discussion of the Fifth Principle Task Force was reduced to a workshop named, "Reimagining Governance." The momentum and zeal for the reforms by the Fifth Principle Task Force had run its course.

It is not surprising that the Fifth Principle Task Force was unable to deliver its recommendations. Two efforts, sponsored by the UUA Board during the debate on the Fifth Principle Task Force, countered the spirit and intent of the Task Force.

Consolidation and the Loss of Local Representation

One month after the publication of the Fifth Principle Task Force report, the UUA Board of Trustees launched another initiative to restructure the way the Association is governed. These changes would eventually diminish the power of representative democracy in the denomination and set into motion the circumstances that enabled the charge to be made that UUism is allegedly a bastion of white supremacy.

At its January 2010 meeting, the trustees drafted a bylaws update to reduce the size of the board and create a system of regions as well as a change to the term of elective service for the offices of the president and moderator. The changes described in *UU World* were due to "a desire to bring clearer focus to our national UUA vision and more democracy, accountability, and effectiveness to UUA governance."[16] At its next meeting on February 4, 2010, the board completed its work on its recommendation to reduce the size of the Board of Trustees. There were some good reasons for rethinking the configuration of the national board. A board of 26 members was simply unwieldy and a reduction to

13 members made sense. The proposed board would be composed of 11 at-large trustees, a financial advisor, and a moderator.

The proposed bylaws change also impacted how the new at-large trustees were to be identified. At that time, the UUA Board was composed of representative trustees identified and elected from the then 19-district configuration of the Association. I knew my UUA Trustee, spoke with her at church and discussed "what was going on in Boston." Henceforth, a Nominating Committee would identify board candidates with the explicit intention to bring greater diversity to the board. *UU World* reported that the Nominating Committee "shall endeavor to nominate individuals so that the membership of the Board of Trustees and each elected committee reflects the full diversity of the Association, especially in regard to historically marginalized communities, but also balancing amongst size of congregation, lay and ordained, geography, age (including youth and young adults), and gender among others."[17] Nearly a decade after this change, the success of the Nominating Committee to fulfill its charter is worth evaluating. Perhaps the Nominating Committee has achieved diversity based on race and gender, but what of diversity of viewpoint? Has the Nominating Committee simply become a gatekeeper to ensure the ideological homogeneity of board members? We at the Fifth Principle Project think that this is exactly what has happened. Furthermore, with the consolidation of the Association's district configuration into five regions and the elimination of local, district-centric trustees, UUA at-large trustees simply lost local visibility and relevance. They could no longer be relied on to hear the voices of everyday UUs.

These consequences were surely not intended in 2010 as the board deliberated their governance bylaws changes. Rather the board, cognizant that the Unitarian Universalist Association was approaching its fiftieth anniversary in 2011, was focused on "[W]hat is necessary for our faith to flourish?" It concluded that a fundamental shift in governance was required, defining governance to mean the setting of expectations, delegation of power, verification of performance and accountability.[18]

There had been earlier efforts to restructure the Association's governance. Five different task forces had labored over a 50-year period reviewing the Association's governance structure and all reached the same conclusion, that the governance was too complex. The board observed, "The time for task forces and study groups is over. We do not need another report. What we need are changes that will clarify roles, engage democratic participation, and align our movement around clear, common goals and values. And those changes have already begun. As the Fifth Principle Task Force report noted, 'Our Association is a system in change.'"[19]

District presidents were included in the conversation, the change was consistent with the shift to regionalization; and, more importantly, the change was occurring at the height of enthusiasm for the transformation of a newly configured and more democratic General

Assembly. The board concluded, "The UUA Board dreams of a time when General Assembly is less about making statements and more about joining lived experience to lived experience and multiplying the power between us and beyond us."[20]

The bylaws changes came up for a vote at the Plenary V session at the 2011 General Assembly in Charlotte, North Carolina.[21] The first voice to speak was at the con mike, Dick Burkhart from the Church of the Larger Fellowship and Board Secretary of UUs for Just Economic Community (UUJEC). Speaking on behalf of UUJEC, he supported the reduction of the size of the board but objected to the nominating committee process for the selection of the slate of trustee delegates. "We want more delegate choice, not the selection by a nominating committee. Remember that this morning we elected new UUA committee members without a single competitive race. We can do better than an inbred power structure."

As it turned out the lofty goals of "more democracy" did not match on-the-ground realities. There was open concern that the board would have too much power through the nominating process over the selection of the 11 at-large board members. The UUA moderator opined, "I can see people's discomfort about the board appointing the Nominating Committee that then nominates the board." Surprisingly the initial draft of the process had a good number of the Nominating Committee members appointed by the board.[22] This shortcoming was corrected in a later revision, but this initial draft does reveal a leadership desire to control the composition of the Board of Trustees. The sponsors of this process did not hide their intention to influence the composition of the board sharing that, "Our highest concern is that we keep diversity . . . The Nominating Committee has to be the guarantee of that diversity."[23]

This call for diversity was not without merit or support. The next speaker at the Plenary session in Charlotte stood at the pro mike and proclaimed, "I support the proposed amendment to replace a monocultural board with a rainbow board." The proposed changes to the board structure, introduction of a nominating committee, and related bylaws changes passed at the 2011 Charlotte General Assembly.

There is a virtue in diversity and democracy. They are not mutually exclusive. The question is, why has our leadership, for more than a decade, failed to trust everyday UUs and the power of our principled democracy to achieve a collective desire for denomination-wide diversity?

The Diversity Conundrum

We've been doing this for a long time. As liberals, we are inclined to self-reflection and unafraid of self-criticism, knowing that such introspection will make our denomination better and help us live more fully in harmony with our principles. In many ways, we are constantly in motion seeking how to form a more perfect union. That was the spirit at the 1997 Phoenix General Assembly when the resolution

"Toward an Anti-Racist Unitarian Universalist Association" was passed.[24] The first objective of that resolution was:

> BE IT FURTHER RESOLVED that the General Assembly urges the Unitarian Universalist Association, its congregations, and community organizations to develop an ongoing process for the comprehensive institutionalization of anti-racism and multiculturalism, understanding that whether or not a group becomes multi-racial, there is always the opportunity to become antiracist. Early steps toward anti-racism might include using curricula such as Journey Toward Wholeness for all age groups, forming racial justice committees, and conducting anti-racism workshops.

There were many earlier efforts to formally achieve racial awareness and multiculturalism.[25] Today, much work is conducted under the umbrella of ARAOMC (anti-racism, anti-oppression, and multiculturalism). Yet despite two decades of earnest striving, we arrived on April 3, 2017 with a self-assessment by the UUA Board of Trustees that the entire denomination was allegedly based on white supremacy culture and was rife with racism and oppression. We have still not found the formula to achieve our diversity goal.

Contributing to the problem is the elephant in the room, that is, diversity goals have never really been well articulated. Enticingly lofty aspirations have motivated our actions, but the lack of clarity has restricted our progress. Breaking this impasse would require an open and honest conversation on the underlying assumptions behind our diversity objective. The failure to have such a conversation is why we've been doing this for such a long time.

Rather, we are reaping what we have sown. We have institutionalized a process, through the Nominating Committee, that has disconnected our governing Board of Trustee members from the voices of local, everyday UUs. Our annual General Assembly remains as "broken" as it was in 2009 to conduct the business of the Association. Our democratic governing spirit has atrophied. We at the Fifth Principle Project still have the highest expectation that ordinary, everyday UUs have the heart and will to achieve our loftiest goals. To be successful, all voices must be heard.

Birth of the Fifth Principle Project

Alarmed by this ever-increasing drift away from the use of democracy in the governance of the denomination's affairs, the Fifth Principle Project was formed. The Fifth Principle Project is a grassroots initiative to gather into community Unitarian Universalists who want to reinvigorate the right of conscience and renew the democratic process in the governance of our denomination.

The Project was started in January 2020. This grassroots movement was initiated by a mass emailing to more than 1,000 congregations seeking the support of others who are like-minded in their desire to regain our democratic footing. Our message stated that only by exercising our collective voting power can we have a voice in setting the direction of our faith movement.

We received a fair amount of support intermingled with some accusations that we "were out of covenant." Although our mass mailing had about a 40% open rate, we did not hear back from many of the 400 people who opened our communication. One response we did not expect was from the Commission on Institutional Change (COIC) which was in its third year in preparation of its report *Widening the Circle of Concern*. The response was indirect, but it was clear our January 6 email caught someone's attention. A January 24, 2020 COIC blog posting entitled "Call for Reflection on the Fifth Principle Task Force Report" opened with the following.

> We are aware that many congregations have been contacted about reinvigorating our Associational conversation about our democratic process and the fifth principle. Ten years ago, there was a task force that prepared a report for the UUA Board of Trustees about these concerns. We would encourage all of you to read this report located here: [the link provided now returns a Page Not Found error].[26]

Concurrent with the mass mailing we established a website, FifthPrincipleProject.org. The website enables people to join this grassroots effort and has been a portal for the discussion of topics germane to the re-enfranchising of our voices. It's time that we get serious about democratically governing ourselves. The alternative is to rescind our Fifth Principle.

3.   COIC: Widening the Circle of Concern

In the wake of the resignation of Rev. Peter Morales as the UUA President, on April 3, 2017 the UUA Board of Trustees established the Commission on Institutional Change (COIC). The board gave the COIC two explicit charges: (1) "analyze structural racism and white supremacy within the UUA" and (2) conduct an "audit of the operation of white privilege and the structure of power within Unitarian Universalism." These charges of white supremacy and structural racism in the denomination were quite serious. The COIC now had the burden of substantiating these charges, especially to a wide audience of skeptical UUs.

At the June 2020 virtual General Assembly, the Commission on Institutional Change released its final report, entitled *Widening the Circle of Concern*. The report contained more than 200 pages and took three years to write. Yet despite the undoubtedly sincere efforts of commission members, the report failed to meet its burden to substantiate the serious charges leveled at the denomination. With failures over a range of evaluation criteria, it is hard to judge the report in any kindlier terms. Nonetheless, the UUA Board is aggressively proceeding forward with the implementation of the report's recommendations as though it is free of shortcomings and beyond

33

scrutiny. The COIC report with its recounting of the pervasiveness of white supremacy, racism, and oppression within the denomination is now the official position of our UU leadership. See Chapter 4, "COIC: Scope and Implications" for more details.

Scholarship

From the start, the COIC report lost its claim to creditability based on the scholarship used as the basis for the report. That is, the COIC modeled its approach on scholarship that has some popular acceptance in university humanities studies. This new scholarship eschews the standard research rigor of forming a hypothesis, gathering data, testing that hypothesis, and then drawing a conclusion on the validity of the hypothesis. Rather, a new epistemology, having to do with how we create knowledge, has found acceptance that is not reason or logic-based but is ideologically based. In this new way of discovering knowledge, an ideological belief is the starting point for both the hypothesis and the conclusion. Everything in between simply reaffirms the ideological belief.

In 2018 three academics working under the heading of The Grievance Studies demonstrated that the scholarship used in the COIC report can readily be manipulated to draw any conclusion desired. To test their theory, the academics wrote and submitted articles to a variety of professional journals. Seven of their articles were published. Their articles, however, were entirely fictitious and devoid of any underlying data or research. One published article, "Human Reactions to Rape

34

Culture and Queer Performativity at the Dog Park," relied on the work of a fictional researcher, Helen Wilson, who was hired by an equally fictitious agency called the Portland Ungendering Research Initiative. Wilson, per the article, spent a year at Portland dog parks where she carefully recorded dogs humping. After "closely and respectfully" examining the genitals of nearly ten thousand dogs she concluded that dog parks were "oppressive spaces that lock both humans and animals into hegemonic patterns of gender conformity that effectively resist bids for emancipatory change." Despite the bogus nature of the premise and data, the article passed peer review and was published. The journal editors even gave the study a rave review stating that the article was "an important contribution to feminist animal geography." The academics worked under the assumption that if an article contained the conclusions and facts desired by an audience, their work would go unchallenged.[27]

Such is the case with the COIC report. The charge given to the COIC began with the premise that white supremacy, racism, and oppression were already present in UUism. Consider an alternate COIC charge, devoid of ideological dogma. "Determine if UUism is based on white supremacy." However, the Board of Trustees was not interested in "if" white supremacy existed; it simply held the belief that white supremacy, racism, and oppression were at the core of UUism.

Theology

A theme, almost a glue, that runs through the COIC report is theology. From the context of the report, theology is meant as a study of religious beliefs rather than the study of God. Chapter 7 of this book, "New UU Orthodoxy" has an in-depth review of liberatory theology and a broader discussion of the ideologies influencing UU leadership. Only one thought on the new UU theology is included in this chapter.

The "Theology" section of the COIC report provides a confusing account of its understanding of our Unitarian and Universalist heritages. It first offers a rather glowing account of our heritages before pivoting to a rather muddled counterargument. The argument starts with the statement that Universalism believes that a loving God would never condemn any portion of humanity to eternal damnation. It comments that Unitarians long held to the established tradition of discerning truth based on facts, reason, and investigation. "Our religious ancestors believed not only in the ability of each of us to discover our own truth but also in the ability to find real truth in the context of our lives as well as in sacred texts and scriptures. This is the basis for our commitment to non-creedalism and aversion to dogma."[28]

Notwithstanding these affirming statements, the report makes a clumsy pivot and argues that despite the glowing nature of our religious heritages, a new UU theology is required as a much-needed improvement. The thrust of the argument is that there is an inherent deficiency in an individually-centered search for truth and meaning.

Therefore, in the search for truth and meaning, a shift to a communal-based locus is required with an additional need to hold individuals accountable.

> Freedom of belief promotes diversity of thought in our communities and fuels the responsible search for truth and meaning that leads toward beloved community . . . Yet over the decades since the consolidation of Unitarians and Universalists, an over emphasis on individual exploration and experience as the primary, if not sole center of religious experience developed.
>
> This centering of the individual decenters the communal as a locus of theological exploration. One of the unintended consequences has been the atomized individualism of the search for truth and meaning without accountability to its impact in communities.[29]

Debate on the pluses and minuses of individualism is a worthy endeavor. The COIC has conveniently, however, concluded that the debate is over and that an individual's search for truth and meaning must be placed in a communal container (whatever that is).

Methodology

With the COVID-19 virus pandemic that has held our nation and others around the world hostage, we have all become acutely aware of the need for a rigorous methodology to collect data in clinical trials so that a safe and effective vaccine can be developed. In the end, among the competing manufacturers, a choice will be made based on a public review of empirical data collected during those trials. We would expect no less.

Unfortunately, if we asked the same question of the COIC on the rigor of their research we would find the answer wanting. Bear in mind, the COIC report is the basis for a structural change to UUism. UUs should be no less demanding of our denominational leadership than we are of our public health officials.

The methodology used by the COIC to gather data was storytelling, also referred to as lived experience. The approach of using storytelling to gather knowledge is consistent with the tenets of postmodernism and the critical theories that emerged from that body of thought. Those theories view society as a collection of identity groups interacting in a labyrinth of social constructs that are, in practice, designed to perpetuate the power of white men. Identity groups are positioned to either serve or benefit from these social constructs. This positionality dictates how one perceives society. The argument continues that those who are positioned to be marginalized have knowledge that is not available to those in positions of power or that such knowledge is available to those in power but is ignored. Therefore, the only way to gain the knowledge needed to eradicate racism is to remove straight white men from the production of knowledge, "center" the voices of those who have been oppressed and gather their stories/knowledge.

Championing the idea of listening to the voices of those who have not been heard is a good thing! We could all be better informed and enriched. However, the COIC is blunt in its assessment that not all voices are to be heard and that it will select which voices will be heard. Furthermore, other methods of discovery such as logic, reason, and science have been rejected since these methods are deemed tools used to perpetuate white supremacy.

This disdain for logic as a tool of white supremacy culture by our UU leadership is not theoretical. In its August 16, 2019 letter of censure to Rev. Dr. Todd Eklof regarding the distribution of his book *The Gadfly Papers*, the Unitarian Universalists Ministers' Association (UUMA) wrote, "We understand from your book that you want to encourage robust and reasoned debate about the direction of our faith. However, we cannot ignore the fact that **logic** has often been employed in white supremacy culture to stifle dissent, minimize expressions of harm, and to require those who suffer to prove the harm by that culture's standards."[30] (bold added)

With storytelling selected as the data-gathering methodology, the COIC stepped on a slippery slope. "[T]he Commission issued calls for testimony and examples of innovation. These calls were issued repeatedly throughout our three years of collecting data. Testimony took the form of individual interviews and submitted testimony. While many were ready to participate and provide their personal testimony, we also heard from folks unwilling to participate."[31]

We do not have any insight on the number of individuals who declined to participate or why they declined. The report offered, "Some expressed experiences too painful to be relived; others were resigned, having shared their stories at other moments of our denominational history and had their voices silenced."[32] What we can conclude is that individuals who did participate self-selected their participation. Self-selection of participants in a data pool automatically skews the results, overemphasizing the stories of individuals who may have a personal or vested interest in portraying UUism as racist and oppressive.

Although the methodology was focused on identity groups, individuals provided the stories. We know that the recounting of a story is influenced both by a person's perspective of the experience and by external concurrent events. For example, the angst, anger, and social media outbursts from the failed hiring decision for the Southern Region Director could indeed have influenced the stories told, either due to a person's direct involvement or to their perception of the event. It does not appear that any such analysis was applied to the stories collected.

Regardless of the context in which a lived experience is incorporated into a person's personal history, that lived experience, as real as it may be held by the individual, may not reflect the actual event. Dr. Dori Laub, an Israeli-American psychiatrist and psychoanalyst, an expert in the area of testimony methodology, is known for collecting testimonies from Holocaust survivors. The following is a frequently cited reference regarding the accuracy of a lived experience from Laub's work. The event was described by a survivor of the October 7, 1944 uprising at Auschwitz, a Nazi death camp. In the survivor's lived experience testimony, she recounted seeing four chimneys being blown up when in reality only one chimney was destroyed.[33] The discrepancy between the lived experience and the actual event does not diminish the impact of this personal experience, but does raise the level of caution needed when evaluating the accuracy of an account of a lived experience.

Perhaps one best practice that does not need explanation in testimony gathering is the care required in formulating interview questions. We are all familiar with the infamously loaded question, "So when did you stop kicking your dog?" Use of a loaded or leading question will skew results. Unfortunately, the COIC did not temper its bias in the questions used to collect testimonial data. Consider one question: "In what ways have you or your group or community been hurt by current racist and culturally biased attitudes and practices within Unitarian Universalism?"[34] Not surprisingly, the report concluded that "[t]he vast majority of people of color and others from identities marginalized within Unitarian Universalism had experienced discriminatory and oppressive incidents or cultures within Unitarian Universalist circles."[35]

This claim, and others in the report, cannot be verified since the collected data was not included in the report. The UUA Board of Trustees deemed that testimonial data was too sensitive to be released and "decided to hold the recordings, documents, and other materials from public view for a period of five years." After that time period, the data will not be publicly released but will be made available for academic use.[36] This decision effectively shields the COIC data from any independent review and leaves the commission free to draw whatever conclusions they desire, conclusions that cannot effectively be challenged.

Avatars - Composite Narratives

With the board's decision to deny access to testimonial data, the COIC provided composite or representative narratives called avatars as a stand-in for raw data. Five avatars were provided: Lay Leader of Color, Minister of Color, Religious Professional of Color, White Accomplice, and White Counter Narrative. However, this substitution of raw data by composite narratives only compounds an already flawed report. Let us remind ourselves that *Widening the Circle of Concern* is an advocacy document and not an analysis of the impact, if any, of white supremacy on UUism. Employing composite narratives opens the COIC to a criticism that the avatars are composed of cherry-picked data, assembled to reinforce the overall narrative that liberal UUism is racist and oppressive. The decision to seal testimonial data created a two-edged sword. One, reviewers cannot challenge the report's conclusion and two, the COIC cannot defend itself from allegations that its avatars are fictional and only loosely based on actual data. It's a mess!

Despite these shortcomings, two composite narratives are reviewed below.

Lay Leader of Color Avatar

This avatar, the first in the report, is found in a section entitled "Hospitality and Inclusion." This section postulates that even Welcoming Congregations "without particular practices" will continue to harm people of color and other marginalized groups. It postulates that if we are inhospitable to one group of people, we are unwelcoming to all.

This avatar is a fictional person given the name Mallory Ramesh. Mallory is 35 years old, Indian, queer, and a social activist. Mallory was attracted to a UU congregation after seeing information on the congregation's website about it being a Welcoming Congregation. The Welcoming Congregation Program was initiated at the 1989 General Assembly to help UU congregations be intentionally welcoming to gay, lesbian, bisexual, queer, and transgender people. At first, Mallory felt uncomfortable at the congregation's book club because every time a topic involving a person of color was raised, Mallory was the go-to person. Despite being new, Mallory was asked to become a congregational leader. Mallory joined the board. Mallory's interest in the White Supremacy Teach-In was not widely shared. At a board meeting, Mallory asked how the board planned to implement the recommendations of the White Supremacy Teach-In, adopt a proposed eighth principle[37] and conduct a congregation-wide racism audit.

Mallory recounted, "The board secretary, a white woman, immediately centered herself and her own discomfort, framing the situation as an attack on herself by me. The issue was left unresolved at the end of the meeting and it was extremely uncomfortable for me." Mallory's relationship with the board members soured. Mallory stopped attending Sunday service, dropped out of the book club, and stopped attending any congregation.[38]

To review, the congregation openly advertised and followed through on its commitment as a Welcoming Congregation. Beyond fulfilling expectations regarding being a Welcoming Congregation, Mallory was valued as an individual and invited to join the congregation's leadership team. A point of friction arose, however, between Mallory and the congregation's board over the Black Lives Unitarian Universalists (BLUU) sponsored White Supremacy Teach-In. This teach-in was originally launched by the UUA Board of Trustees when it declared that UUism fostered white supremacy, racism, and oppression. Mallory stated that there was reluctance by some congregation leaders to participate in the teach-in and further lamented that the commitment by the congregation was limited to a single service and a reflection.

We can now see how manipulation can be introduced when a fictional narrative is used as a substitute for real data. We are left with the implicit statement, voiced by Mallory, but written by the COIC, that if anyone is reluctant to participate in the teach-in they are automatically considered to be "wrong." The BLUU Teach-in was an extension of the declaration that UUism fosters white supremacy. Both were controversial and disagreement should not be unexpected.

In the end, we really know nothing of the dynamics between Mallory, the local church board and the congregation. We may also view this Mallory avatar as a proxy for UUA authoritarian control. Mallory's frustration that the outgoing minister and incoming interim minister were not moving forward with UU leadership initiatives such as a proposed eighth principle and racism audit is, at its best, impatience, or more accurately a disregard for congregational polity, the ability of congregations to self-govern their affairs. The implication being that if a congregation questions the implementation of UUA leadership initiatives, that congregation is "wrong."

White Counter Narrative Avatar

This avatar is in a section entitled "Innovations and Risk-Taking." The naming of the avatar as a "counter narrative" reveals the thinking of the Commission on Institutional Change that it has "the correct narrative" and that anything not in alignment with its point of view is wrong and should be dismissed.

This counter narrative avatar was given the fictional name John E. Pickett and supposedly is representative of a white heterosexual male. Age is unknown. The John avatar unloads on the COIC stating he has shared his "dismay at the direction that our beloved Association is heading by adopting dangerous authoritarian ideas like critical race

45

theory/critical race theology, rejecting logic, and promoting dangerous and disrespectful persons to leadership." John conveys the work he and others have done in advancing civil rights, that his personal medical professionals are all from multicultural backgrounds, that his daughter shattered gender norms by becoming a pilot and that he worked to call the first openly gay Director of Religious Education. He also laments the troubling idea being pushed by the Commission regarding "cultural misappropriation," sharing that his congregation happily celebrated Day of the Dead and Juneteeth. This avatar concludes with three observations.

One, the current direction of the UUA and groups like the Commission "exacerbates divisions when we should be minimizing differences and focusing on unity." Two, reasonable people of color will not join a faith that stereotypes them with identity politics and Caucasians will not join a church known for harboring white supremacists. Many will leave and the Association will collapse financially. Finally, we must get our faith back in line with the principles of liberalism, democracy and critical thought.[39]

John is never heard from again in the report. More importantly, let's pause for a moment and absorb again the extraordinary claim that the Commission on Institutional Change made in classifying Pickett's avatar as a "counter narrative." The designation of "counter" was intentional and was meant to convey the message "not in alignment with" the vision for UUism as seen by the Commission on Institutional

Change. The COIC excludes from its vision of a new UU orthodoxy a "faith back in line with the principles of liberalism, democracy and critical thought." UUism is heading into a storm of controversy!

Some Sobering Trends and Questionable Facts

The COIC report is at its best when it relies on data and statistics collected by an outside source such as the Pew Research Center.[40] The Pew Research Center observed that fewer people are participating in religious communities. There is an emerging generation that answers the question of religious affiliation as "none." Unitarian Universalism is not immune from this downsizing trend in religious life. Although statistically the Association reports that we have 1,000 congregations, the reality is that only 819 congregations meet the standards to be a congregation.[41] An excellent point is made that those who enter our doors today are not "religious refugees" but are experiencing a faith community for the first time. Additionally, the demographics of the nation are changing with growing numbers of non-whites and those with multicultural roots.

Unfortunately, and more commonly, the COIC report mingles facts with observations positing as factual information. Consider these examples.

"A disturbing new trend is that white leaders who openly speak out about white supremacy culture and the need for change are also finding their employment ended or affected."[42] This charge that the employment of individuals has been impacted or ended is a serious allegation, but no data were presented.

"People of color and others targeted and endangered in this world come into our congregations seeking solace, only to discover that while our beliefs are grounding and life-giving, the ways they are practiced in too many of our communities cause harm, confusion and pain."[43] This observation that people of color and others find harm in some UU congregations is essential to the report's thesis, but for some reason is presented only as an un-footnoted bullet point in the report. It is a powerfully emotive image that begs for further elaboration. Again, no data were presented.

The breadth of the data collected for the report is explained as "more than eighty hours of audio and video recordings and more than 650 pages of documents from more than 1,100 participants."[44] What is not learned from these statistics is exactly how many people actually provided testimonials. Since the report's methodology was based on collected stories, it would seem incumbent upon the COIC to share information on its sample size. For example, it is not known if the 1,100 participants cited in the report included those who provided testimonials as well as those who attended a focus group meeting, took a survey, or participated in some other fashion. It is disconcerting that a basic outline of people who provided testimonial data was not provided. Any report that purports to provide a roadmap for UUism should be free of such structural shortcomings in its information base.

The Demographic Challenge

The COIC report was not the first UUA document to claim that adjusting to changing U.S. demographics is a sound and essential strategy of the denomination. Shortly after assuming the presidency of the Association in 2009, Rev. Morales set into motion the Strategic Review of Professional Ministers, intending to define a "new ministry for a new America." In March 2011 a report from this strategic review was issued in which it was argued that for UUism to thrive there must be a "robust flow of UU religious professionals who are equipped to provide vital ministry in congregations that thrive in a future that is increasingly diverse racially, ethnically and culturally—and who help our faith grow to serve all who yearn for liberal religious community."[45] How did our UU leadership view this new America?

Fortunately, relevant demographic information is hosted on the UUA website. Although the data dates from 2008, the information provides a snapshot of the racial profile of the denomination along with other characteristics. The information provided below is from a document entitled "Unitarian Universalist Demographic Data from the American Religious Identification Survey (ARIS) and the Faith Communities Today (FACT) Survey."[46]

Demographic	1990		2008	
	U.S.	UUs	U.S.	UUs
White	72%	90%	66%	75%
Black	13%	5%	11%	6%
Hispanic	6%	3%	14%	15%
Other	4%	3%	9%	4%

Table 1: Racial and Ethnic Diversity

The data on White UUs from 1990 to 2008 is consistent with general demographic trends showing a shrinking percentage of Whites in the overall U.S. population and a corresponding drop in White UUs from 90% to 75%. The data on Black UUs, however, is inconsistent with observations in the COIC report, showing an increase of 5% to 6%. The largest percentage increase was seen in Hispanic UUs (3% to 15%) outpacing the overall U.S. population growth (6% to 14%). A similar growth pattern in Hispanic membership was also seen among evangelical Protestants, mainline Protestants, and Catholics.[47]

The most dramatic downturn in UUism was its tolerance for political diversity. In 1990 the ratio of Democrats to Republicans was 2:1, 18 years later, that ratio was 11:1. The takeaway that UUs skew to the Democrat side of the political spectrum may be of comfort to some, but does present visitors with an uncomfortable environment if their views do not align with liberal political thinking.

Without question, however, UUs are on a demographic island when it comes to levels of education and religious beliefs. The 2008 ARIS/FACT report showed that UUs were better educated than the general population with more than 50% of UUs having a college or post-graduate education, compared to only 25% of the general U.S. population. This observation was consistent with a 2014 study of 30 U.S. religious groups that listed Unitarian Universalism as the second most educated denomination, ranked just behind Hindus.[48] UUs also significantly diverge from the U.S. population on the matter of religious beliefs. Fifty-eight percent of UUs considered themselves secular or somewhat secular compared to only 16% of the general U.S. population.

In the end, discussions on racial demographics may very well be moot. The run-away demographic, mentioned earlier, that may offer UUism growth, diversity in racial make-up, and diversity in thought and longevity are the "nones," those with no religious affiliation. Consider a 2018 Pew Research Center report entitled "Why America's 'nones' don't identify with religion." The report disclosed that the number one reason why "nones" do not favor a religious affiliation is that they "question a lot of religious teaching." The next three reasons were "don't like the position churches take on social/political issues," "don't like religious organizations," and "don't believe in God."[49] It is beyond the scope of this book to continue this discussion on demographics. It may be observed that the COIC report was so heavily invested in white supremacy and racial identity that it failed to take a broader view of demographic trends that could bring more diversity to UUism.

Read Despite Flaws

Bottom line, *Widening the Circle of Concern* is heavily flawed. These flaws, however, seem to be of little concern to our UU leadership and, quite honestly, of no concern to ordinary UUs. Of course, concerns of ordinary UUs can only be raised if the report is read.

The report is unnecessarily long and full of convoluted language that is a barrier to reading. One reviewer observed that the language is numbingly bureaucratic, citing this example, "We used an action-based research methodology that involved collection of materials, analysis and two outside consultants." A more readable alternative was offered, "We did research and used two consultants." There is an introduction but no executive summary. The Introduction speaks to the charge given to the COIC, its purpose and goals, etc., but provides no summary of findings or a summary of proposed actions. Rather, throughout the report there is a sprinkling of statements, take aways and recommendations/actions. This scattering of observations makes it difficult to assemble the data into a coherent narrative. Appendix II of the report does provide a summary of the report's more than 30 recommendations and over 110 actions, but no guidance on how to proceed on these recommendations and actions.

One mechanism provided to introduce the report to UU's is an eleven-session online study guide provided on the UUA website. The sessions are built around the structure of the report. The study guide, unfortunately, does not provide any summarized interpretations of the report. Participants are simply asked to read particular sections of the report as a preparatory step for each study session. In each session, supplemental readings or information are offered which at times are germane and other times a bit odd. In the session regarding the report's Restoration and Reparation section, a link is provided to the *Feeling Wheel* by the Gottman Institute, which appears to be a family and couples counseling company. The most substantive part of each study session is the discussion questions. The discussion questions are constructed to tie back to specific themes in the report. The study guide is a noble effort but does not overcome the cumbersome wording of the report, which is its main barrier to reading.

We attended all of the sessions at the 2020 virtual General Assembly when the report was presented, and we found the coverage cursory at best. Credit is given to the commission for establishing several distribution channels. There are three free versions. A web-based version of the report is found at UUA.org; you can find it by searching for *Widening the Circle of Concern*. The web version includes an audio reading of each section. A printer-friendly version can be downloaded, as well as a copy of the report in PDF format. The report can be purchased in book format from the UU Book and Gift Shop, inSpirit, for $16.00. A copy of the report was sent to each congregation.

We encourage all UUs to read the report despite the flaws and length. It is critical that UUs become fully aware of the substantive changes envisioned for UUism outlined in this report.

4. COIC: Scope and Implications

Months before the public release of the report by the Commission on Institutional Change, *Widening the Circle of Concern*, the UUA Board of Trustees was already making preparations for the implementation of the report's recommendations. In many ways, the board was exhibiting behaviors we want in a governing body. There was a commitment to make sure that this change effort would not fail. The board even offered itself to be the change model for congregations.[50] Now was the time to "set a true road map" for the denomination. The COIC report was to be that road map. However, the COIC report can be considered less as a road map for the future of Unitarian Universalism and more as a warning of the extent to which an external ideology has taken root in UU leadership thinking.

As laudable as the intentions of the UUA Board may have been, the problem is that the board is operating in a self-fulfilling feedback loop. First the board self-declared that UUism was based on white supremacy and was thus inherently racist and oppressive. Then the UUA board created a commission to confirm its own declaration. Finally, the board committed to implementing its own commission's recommendations to solve the board's self-proclaimed problem of UUism's white supremacy.

While many UUs support social justice programs focused on anti-racism, anti-oppression, and multiculturalism (ARAOMC), those programs have now become fused to the denomination's alleged white supremacy nature. Can an individual UU support ARAOMC without also agreeing that UUism is based on white supremacy? What is the appeal of a revision of our principles motivated solely to rectify UUism's alleged white supremacy nature?

These questions are raised because with the publication of the COIC report, action is now underway that will require UUs to either agree or disagree with the board's white supremacy declaration. At the 2022 General Assembly, a vote is planned to determine if UUs want to advance anticipated revisions to Article II based on COIC recommendations as drafted by the Article II Study Commission. Another finalizing vote is planned for the 2023 General Assembly. The changes, not yet known, could be sweeping, since the Article II Study Commission has been given wide freedom to revamp all sections of Article II as well as consider a new eighth principle.[51]

Those far-off votes could easily be relegated to a priority of "I'll worry about that tomorrow." The UUA Board, however, is moving forward now. At its September 14, 2020 Zoom meeting, the UUA Board formalized its commitment to the COIC recommendations by unanimously adopting a resolution that read in part:

Whereas systemic racism and white supremacy culture exist in many Unitarian Universalist institutions;

Whereas the UUA Board of Trustees appointed the Commission on Institutional Change in 2017;

Whereas the UUA Board of Trustees accepted their report ("Widening the Circle of Concern") in June 2020;

Whereas there has been an unfortunate pattern of reports received without actions taken in the history of Unitarian Universalism, especially with regard to equity, diversity, inclusion and anti-racism . . .

The UUA Board then resolved to collaborate with a new Accountability Group that will oversee the implementation of COIC-inspired changes through 2025.[52] A month later at the October 15, 2020 board meeting, the COIC Implementation Mission Alignment Team (CIMAT) was introduced. CIMAT is a senior leadership organizational structure charged with facilitating the implementation of COIC changes into the operations of the Association's governing bodies and staff.

Scope of COIC Recommendations

The recommendations in the COIC report, summarized in the report's Appendix II, are organized according to the structure of the report with recommendations and action steps for theology, governance, congregations and communities, hospitality, and inclusion and so on. The recommendations are sweeping, reaching into every nook and cranny of the denomination.

The major focus of the recommended actions is to rectify UUism's alleged oppression of Black, Indigenous and people of color. Recommended actions include "consult with identity-based groups" to establish "accountable relationships with Black, Indigenous and people of color." "Study the reparations movement and examine implications for institutions at all levels of Unitarian Universalism." UU-based advocacy groups such as DRUUM, TRUUst, and EqUUal Access[53] are specifically called upon to develop certification programs for congregations. Likewise, it is recommended that the Welcoming Congregation program be revised to emphasize diversity and anti-oppression. A new Promising Practices program is envisioned to recognize congregations that have become more equitable, inclusive, and diverse.

Despite the outer appeal of greater diversity, none of the recommendations are presented as optional. In the "Governance" section it is recommended that the regional organization structure be employed as a watchdog to determine which "regions are working well and address those that are not" in the spread of the UU leadership's new policies. The consequences for any congregation failing a regional evaluation on its adoption of UU leadership policies are left vague and unarticulated. The lack of specificity regarding the consequence of non-compliance is of little comfort. UUA bylaws and rules may be modified regarding the yearly certification of congregations to make such certification dependent upon some level of compliance. New congregations requesting membership into the Association might be subject to a compliance rigor not faced by existing member congregations. Article III, covering membership in the Association, grants the UUA Board a substantial prerogative. "The Board of Trustees shall adopt rules to carry out the intent" of member admission.

The concept of covenanting is frequently mentioned as a mechanism to integrate the policies in the COIC report into the mission and goals of regions and congregations. "Incorporate principles of covenant into anti-oppression work across all UU organizations." Covenant, in this context, does not convey the sense of "agreement" but rather the more weaponized version used by those who advocate for the COIC policies to ensure compliance. How one may interpret the scope or design of a UU leadership compliance review is not the question to ponder. The very fact that a compliance mechanism is being considered regarding the adoption of UU-leadership-designed policies is an alarming departure from traditional practices. Such an approach also conflicts with congregational autonomy and congregational polity.

Administrative or Theological Center

Less obvious in a reading of the *Widening the Circle of Concern* is the intent by our Boston-based UU leadership to greatly expand its power and influence over the denomination. We can all agree that Boston is the administrative center of the denomination. The Association's member congregations grant our UU leadership specific authority to carry out the primary mission of the Association which is to serve the needs of the member congregations.

The COIC report makes clear the intent of our UU leadership to also assume the mantle of a theological center. The COIC report asserts that "Acknowledgement of anti-oppression work as a theological mandate is essential."[54] The concept of an ecclesiastical power center that can issue theological mandates is disconcerting and incompatible with local congregational autonomy and congregational polity. To be clear, simply saying that one has a theological mandate does not necessarily make it so, no matter how poetically it may be stated. The report also states, "As a people of faith, our call to collective justice work, through accountable partnerships, is our salvific path."[55]

Unlike the clarity in the power granted to our UU leadership to conduct the business of the Association, there is no clarity or evidence that member congregations or UUs in general have conferred any ecclesiastical power on our UU leadership. When we permit UU leadership to self-authorize by claiming the power of a higher authority, no matter the merit of the goal, we establish a dangerous precedent in denominational governance. Consider the consequences when administrative and ecclesiastical powers are consolidated. Empowered with a theological mandate and enabled by the Association's bureaucracy, the ability to impose rules and requirements on UUs and member congregations becomes a reality. Of course, this reality, regardless of our leadership's desire for consolidated power, can be thwarted by the independence of our local autonomous congregations. It is not surprising then that the COIC report made clear an intention to reduce the autonomy of congregations and redefine congregational polity, the system of governance upon which congregations derive their independence.

Governance

"When we talk about governance, we are talking about power."[56] This sentence opens the section of the COIC report entitled "Governance." The clarity of this sentence is a welcome relief from the convoluted language that generally characterizes the report. As noted earlier, the ideology of Critical Race Theory with its preoccupation with power had an influence on the Commission on Institutional Change. Not surprisingly we find references to power in the COIC report. We are assured, for instance, that avatar reenactments, although devoid of details such as dates and identities, maintain "context, power dynamics and impacts."[57] Among the Governance recommendations is an action to "Articulate the tools of power analysis that enable leaders to understand and rebalance power at all levels of Unitarian Universalism."

Congregational Autonomy

Problematic in the COIC report is a recommendation regarding congregational autonomy that goes to the heart of our congregation's independence. The report considered changes to Article XIII, C-13.4, Autonomy, in our Association's bylaws. At present this article reads:

> Each district or region shall be autonomous and shall be controlled by its own member congregations to the extent consistent with the promotion of the welfare and interests of the Association as a whole and of its member congregations.

The report takes particular aim at the phrase "consistent with the promotion of the welfare and interests of the Association." VISIONS Inc, a consulting firm employed by the COIC, asked if language could be developed that more explicitly tied "the welfare and interests of the Association" to UU leadership efforts regarding the dismantling of systems of power and privilege.

VISIONS also questioned whether a change could be made in section C-2.2. in Article II called Inclusion to provide more leverage to the UU leadership in its pursuit to root out UUism's alleged white supremacy culture. "Might acknowledging inequity, white supremacy culture and addressing it be added here?"[58] The history of how this Inclusion section came to be added to Article II will be discussed in more detail in Chapter 5, "Article II Study Commission: Story of Our Principles." It is sufficient for now to point out that the language in this section, which dates back to a failed attempt to change Article II in 2009, is the first time ideological language was proposed for our Association's bylaws. The Inclusion section reads in part, "Systems of power, privilege, and oppression have traditionally created barriers for persons and groups with particular identities, ages, abilities, and histories."

VISIONS then questioned what the consequences would be if congregations did not adhere to the board's initiative regarding white supremacy and power structures. "If congregations do not adhere to the inclusion bylaw, what might be the consequences?"

After wrestling with options such as bylaws changes and the development of rules or policies, it was finally recommended that it may be "more utilitarian to create a policy related to DEI [diversity, equity and inclusion], than to refer to the separate policy from the bylaws."

Although everyday UUs are not versed in Association bylaws, rules, or policies, our UU leadership is quite fluent in such matters. The nature of UUism can be refocused with incremental adjustments and amendments to our bylaws and rules of governance. UUs should be aware of suggested changes to our principles and sources, but also of other changes to our bylaws offered by our UU leadership.

Congregational Polity

Congregational polity is a form of church government from which our local congregations derive their independence and freedom to self-govern. Congregational polity was affirmed in the 1961 Constitution of the newly formed Unitarian Universalist Association.

> The Unitarian Universalist Association hereby declares and affirms the independence and autonomy of local churches, fellowships and associate members;

> and nothing in this Constitution or in the By-Laws of
> the Association shall be deemed to infringe upon the
> congregational polity of churches and fellowships . .
> .[59]

The spirit of this language continues today in our Association's bylaws. Conrad Wright, one of UU's notable historians, in his book *Walking Together, Polity and Participation in Unitarian Universalist Churches*, remarked that the tradition of congregational polity has been handed down to us from the Cambridge Platform as envisioned by Massachusetts Bay Puritans three and a half centuries ago. "No doctrine of the church is likely to be acceptable to us which does not acknowledge our continuity with that tradition."[60] Wright goes on to cite another historian, Sidney Mead, who observed that the only things Unitarian Universalists could agree upon were congregational polity and *Robert's Rules of Order*.

The Commission on Institutional Change report, however, takes strong exception to the prevailing notion of congregational polity stating, "we have developed a mythology about how we are governed that claims the complete autonomy of both congregations and individuals within congregations," adding, "This is not what the Cambridge Platform, upon which our polity is based, states."[61] It could be assumed that the argument advanced by the COIC revolves around the notion expressed in the Cambridge Platform as the "communion of Churches one with another." The spirit of this communion was that churches pledged lateral commitment to one another of care, consultation, admonition, participation, recommendation and relief. There was no center, just a web of communion. Wright expressed this concept in contemporary terms as a "community of autonomous congregations."

We should be clear-eyed that this idealized state of communion never actually existed. By 1720 the original 1648 platform had been revised seven times.[62] Our own Unitarian experience added a blow to this hoped-for harmony when our ancestors emerged as a liberal wing and split to form the American Unitarian Association in 1825. One could also argue that the UU-leadership-sponsored change in 2011, by eliminating our district structure in favor of a regional structure that created a stronger centralized UUA, was another contemporary blow to the ideal of a "community of autonomous congregations" and the hoped-for lateral congregational relationships.

This last observation about the damage done to lateral congregational relationships should not be dismissed lightly. With the merging of 19 districts into five regions, monthly meetings of district boards were no longer held, district newsletters ceased publication and annual district gatherings disappeared. For many people, their connection to the UUA was through their district relationships and connections. In October 2019, I (co-author Jay) had the opportunity to participate in a Commission on Appraisal review with six or eight other UUs. The topic of the review was covenant, but the conversation drifted to our personal and congregation's relationship with the UUA. I shared that when the UUA leadership eliminated the districts and our local trustees, "The UUA simply vanished." A commission member, who had been sitting quietly, leaned over toward me and appreciatively whispered, "Thank you for saying that."

Lateral connections were once championed by the 2009 Fifth Principle Task Force. As you may recall among the recommendations made by the Task Force was to physically seat General Assembly delegates in a geographic configuration to achieve a Task Force objective of "Know your neighbor to build UU community & effectiveness beyond the walls of our congregation."

Our current UU leadership, however, is moving in a different direction seeking less decentralization of authority and more concentration of centralized authority. Leadership enthusiasm behind this effort is unmistakable, but the challenge to local autonomy rests solely on a contention, despite decades of practice, that we have a faulty understanding of congregational polity. Consider this comment in the report from an unattributed observer.

> It seems like we as a denomination have to relearn the Cambridge Platform and understand that our congregational polity does not allow us to do just whatever we want.
>
> That there is a relationship between each congregation in the larger movement . . . and **this idea that the UUA can't tell us what to do is bologna**.[63] (bold added)

That last sentence cannot better illuminate the real intent of the COIC and our UU leadership on power consolidation. As shared earlier, there has been a consistent movement by our UU leadership to centralize and aggregate their power. This aggregation of power aligns with a statement once heard from a UU leader declaring that for UUism to be "impactful" we must harness the energies of the denomination. It appears the mechanism selected for this harnessing of the energies of the denomination is through the undoing of our traditions and local autonomy and congregational polity.

One final comment is offered on congregational polity regarding the inherent tension between local independence and the necessity of some level of centralized authority. Again, let Conrad Wright speak to this tension.

> For Unitarians and Universalists, as for other denominations adhering to congregational polity, one result has been an especially acute tension between traditional local independency [sic] and a necessary consolidation of forces and centralized control.
>
> Furthermore, to the long-standing resistance in congregational polity to hierarchy and centralization, there has been added the conflict between ecclesiastical structures and bureaucracy.
>
> The Church as a community of the faithful, and the denomination as a bureaucratic organization, are not the same thing, and there is an ineluctable (inevitable) conflict of values between them. Thus, there are two sources of tension built into our present

polity: parochialism versus denominationalism, and the Church versus bureaucracy.[64]

The 1997 Commission on Appraisal report entitled *Interdependence: Renewing Congregational Polity* offers one way to ease this inherent tension. This report is thoughtful and well-researched and contributes to the overall scholarship of UUism. The report observed that "a renewed theological understanding of religious community . . . is key to reaching a fresh and liberating understanding of congregational polity itself."[65] Having a robust conversation on congregation polity is healthy. Simply declaring that our understanding of congregational polity is wrong is counterproductive.

Who is working for whom?

When we consider any COIC recommendations, we should have clarity about the ultimate sources of accountability and authority for denominational governance. Is the UUA Board of Trustees free to do as it pleases? Recall that the 2009 Fifth Principle Task Force stated, "A central principle of policy-style governance is a board's assurance that it acts as the informed voice of the organization's sources of authority and accountability—its moral owners." The report described the moral owners as the "duly elected and called leaders of the member congregations, and specifically member congregations' delegates to the UUA General Assembly."[66] This clarity, however, was not reflected in the 2020 UUA Board of Trustees orientation packet.[67] In that orientation packet, the board's sources of accountability and authority were listed as:

- Our member congregations
- Current and future generations of Unitarian Universalists
- The heritage, traditions, and ideals of Unitarian Universalism
- The vision of Beloved Community
- The Spirit of life, love, and the holy

The sources from which an organization draws its authority are critical for that organization's legitimacy. Critically, consent must be given by those who are claimed to be a source of authority. Although poetically high-minded, the last three sources of authority cannot grant consent. Nor can "future generations." By virtue of the denomination's representative form of governance, consent can only be granted by congregation delegates who attend General Assembly. This may all sound a bit like tomato or tomahto, but without clarity and without consent, how can a governing body such as the UUA Board of Trustees claim that it is speaking in the name of those governed? Governance is a complicated business, and democratic governance is outright messy. See Chapter 9, "21st Century Fifth Principle" for more information.

Accountability

A recurring theme in the COIC report is accountability. The concept appears as early as the Preface, where it is observed that among the "lamentations and learnings" that "[n]o shared accountability structures and processes are in place to hold people accountable for the continued harming of Black people, Indigenous people, and people of color among us."[68] This observation encapsulates two inter-related themes of "accountability" and "harm." Consider these examples:

- Living into the Power of We . . . holds us accountable to repairing the legacy of theological harm we have perpetrated against some in our community . . .[69]
- Unitarian Universalist congregations and other organizations must also become more skilled at being accountable to groups rather than to individuals.[70]
- Provide learning circles and virtual learning circles for groups of white people interested in learning how to be accountable to Black people, Indigenous people, and people of color and co-journeying with them.[71]

The report applies this concept of accountability with a fair degree of flexibility to cover a wide range of areas, including an intrusion into what many UUs would consider their personal and private relationship with UUism. Consider this reference to our Fourth Principle, a free and responsible search for truth and meaning. The following is from the "Methodology" section of the report, quoted in its entirety to eliminate any doubt of the intent of the COIC.

> As a faith community, we place a high value on the free and responsible search for truth and meaning. Yet this has somehow come to be interpreted almost exclusively through an individualistic lens.
>
> We suggest that as a religious organization, bound together by choice, we operate as a collective based on principle, so that this "free and responsible" search

is done within the **boundaries of communities**.[72] (bold added)

This intent to place boundaries on our Fourth Principle due to the "individualistic lens" of one's search, or, as expressed in the "Theology" section of the report, the "over-emphasis on individual exploration," is a consistent and unmistakable UU leadership objective. Let there be no doubt that there is a clear intent to place an asterisk at the end of our Fourth Principle. Our leadership has been silent on how these boundaries will be set and what will be the consequences if boundaries are breached. The one thing that we know for sure is that UUism simply cannot thrive under the weight of authoritarian oversight over our search for truth and meaning.

Role of President and Moderator

One COIC recommendation on merging the roles of president and moderator into a single elective office merits further study.[73] Today the UUA president is selected in a competitive race that sees candidates go on the stump, visit congregations, pitch their vision, and ask for votes. Candidates then continue the election process with speeches and more handshaking at General Assembly, where the election is held. However, once elected, the president really does not have a great deal of institutional power. The president is on the Board of Trustees but has no vote.

The relationship between the board and president has, at times, been turbulent. When Rev. Peter Morales started his presidency in 2009 a board member greeted the new president by declaring, "The president's vision is irrelevant unless it's also the board's vision."[74]

The moderator, a role established in 1938, is far less visible than the president despite the considerable institutional power that the moderator has. The moderator serves as the Chief Governance Officer of the Association and presides over meetings of the Board of Trustees and General Assembly. The moderator is nominated by the Board of Trustees or by a petition by 50 certified congregations. Both the moderator and president serve six-year terms.[75] At the virtual 2020 General Assembly, Meg Riley and Charles Du Mond were nominated as co-moderators. Since no competing candidates were on the slate, there was no stumping for votes. Per the Association's bylaws, if no competing candidates are nominated, "election" is by affirmation.

Rectifying the imbalance in the visibility in the election of the president and moderator is a step in the right direction. Ensuring that there are competitive races for the most senior positions in the denomination is good democracy. However, fixing one problem and leaving other governance shortcomings unaddressed still leaves the denomination with a serious governance problem. It would be like changing a single flat tire on a car with four flat tires. We need to correct our current situation of governance by an unaccountable at-large Board of Trustee members and the unfinished work to fix our broken General Assembly.

The Public Face

Much can be understood by what people say and what they don't say. The article on the report by the Commission on Institutional Change in the Fall 2020 issue of *UU World*, "Commission on Institutional Change's final report is a critical waypoint, not the end of the journey," reveals much by what it did not say. Assuming that more UUs will read this *UU World* article than the actual report, the article, written by three senior UUA leaders, was an effort to shape the public perception of the COIC report. Absent from the article was any mention of the recurring theme of accountability, even though the report referenced the terms *accountability* or *accountable* over 100 times. The article simply sidestepped the prominence of accountability in the report. There was also an odd rebranding regarding our Second Principle, justice, equity, and compassion in human relations. The *UU World* article opened with an assertion that the COIC "has created a pathway for our faith to collectively move to a new level of embodying the principles of justice, equity, compassion, and liberation." Liberation, liberation theology and liberatory interpretations were terms used in the report to reinforce the underlying assumption that UUism is oppressive. Nor did the article share that the COIC report never actually embraced justice, equity and compassion. Rather diversity, equity, and inclusion were the emphasis of the report, sometimes referenced by the acronym DEI.

The article portrayed the COIC report as a warm-hearted effort that "redeems the essential promise and ideals of Unitarian Universalism."[76] We should not allow ourselves, however, to be distracted by calming words from the fundamental operating assumption of the Commission on Institutional Change: that UUism is allegedly based on white supremacy culture, is oppressive and racist. If we are truly to redeem the essential promise and ideals of Unitarian Universalism, we must not allow this ideological assault on UU's principles of liberalism, democracy, and critical thought to succeed.

Consequences

With the publication of the COIC report, there is now a need for individual UUs to take a stand regarding the discussion on the direction of UUism. With its focus on the COIC recommendations, we are facing more years of UU leadership with its attention turned inward. This is unfortunate. Many people came to UUism because of the denomination's engagement in the public debate on issues such as nuclear disarmament, civil rights, and women's reproductive rights. UUs would agree that engagement on those issues is still needed as well as on other issues, such as income inequality, police reform, gun safety, access to voting, institutional incarceration, immigrant rights and, of course, climate change. Yet the inward focus of the denomination's leadership withdraws the denomination's moral authority from the debate on these issues, rendering our public voice silent.

5.   Article II Study Commission: Story of Our Principles

In late December 2019, six months before the 2020 virtual General Assembly, the UUA Board of Trustees was entertaining a charge to a new board initiative called the Article II Study Commission. The Article II Study Commission is the vehicle by which proposed changes to Article II in the Association's bylaws are drafted and presented at General Assembly. Article II contains our principles, sources, and statements regarding the purpose of the Association, our commitment to inclusion, and a freedom of belief assertion. No other section in the bylaws could be considered more sacred, since Article II holds the spirit and heart of UUism. What should be of concern to UUs is the UUA Board's charge to the Commission that indicates it is "free to revise, replace, or restructure" all sections of Article II. The Commission was further directed to deliver its proposed changes to the UUA Board of Trustees by January 2021. The Commission failed to meet this deadline, but the first vote on changes to Article II is still scheduled to be held at the 2022 General Assembly. If a majority vote in 2022 is secured, a vote will be taken at the 2023 General Assembly to either accept or reject the proposed changes to our principles. A two-thirds majority vote in 2023 is required for the changes to be accepted. The final charge to the Article II Study Commission reflected a December 2019 draft that reads in part:

75

. . . the Principles and Purposes should lead us into the second quarter of the 21st Century, while honoring the historic roots of our liberal, progressive faith.

We therefore charge this commission to root its work in Love as a principal guide in its work; attending particularly to the ways that we (and our root traditions) have understood and articulated Love, and how we have acted out of Love.[77]

Read without knowledge of other concurrent UUA leadership activities, this charge to base the Commission's work on love is warming, embracing, and compelling. Bear in mind, six months later, the same UUA Board of Trustees endorsed the COIC report that condemned UUism as a vehicle for white supremacy, rife with racism and oppression. This is the same Commission on Institutional Change that viewed the "historic roots of our liberal, progressive faith" as mere instruments of white supremacy.

Four Observations About the Article II Study Commission

First, the Article II Study Commission and the Committee on Institutional Change should be viewed as a single coordinated effort under the direction of our UUA Board of Trustees. It is abundantly clear that the individuals behind these efforts have an excellent understanding of the denomination's institutional levers of power. They are well aware, for instance, that by changing the Association's bylaws the impact they want to make on UUism will prevail long after they leave office. Since UU leadership has control over all communication channels, access to the Association's budget, and the ability to set the agenda for General Assembly, it has the wherewithal to succeed.

Second, in the announcement of the Article II Study Commission, there is an assertion that UUism is in an "ethical, moral and spiritual crisis."[78] This assertion that UUism is allegedly in the midst of a crisis is the fundamental rationale for the need to revise our principles. As we established, our ethical, moral, and spiritual crisis is the result of the UUA Board's declaration, after its 90-minute Zoom session in April 2017, that the UUA and the denomination are based on white supremacy. All other events flow from that single decision! The COIC report plumbed the depth of this crisis, observing that "We are on a journey towards redemption. We have lived a year filled with lamentations . . . with the strengths of generations, the failures of everyday, and the deep-down gritty messiness that is the promise of our Salvation."[79] We must, therefore, seek redemption in order to be liberated from our depraved state. "What is at stake is nothing less than the future of our faith."[80]

Let's be clear, UUs are under no obligation to unquestionably accept this declaration of white supremacy. It is, however, essential to UU leadership that their white supremacy declaration remains intact and unchallenged. If this assertion of white supremacy is rejected, then there is no ethical, moral or spiritual crisis. Without this crisis, the prime motivator to reshape our principles simply evaporates.

The third observation is that the concept of accountability was downplayed in the announcement of the Article II Study Commission. Such was not the position taken in the COIC report that asserted that a liberation theology was necessary to "call us to be accountable to the legacies of our past deeds and to work for an equitable future. This will lay the groundwork for our work around truth, transformation and reparations."[81] It is not that accountability was absent from the Article II Study Commission's announcement, rather it was conveyed under the guise of covenant.

The most dramatic and public instance of the consequences of the weaponization of covenant and its accountability implications was the action taken against Rev. Dr. Todd Eklof regarding the distribution of his book *The Gadfly Papers* at the 2019 Spokane General Assembly. We have previously cited the Unitarian Universalist Ministers' Association August 16, 2019 letter of censure, noting the disdain held by the UUMA over Eklof's use of logic. That letter also shows how covenant has been used as a tool to silence voices and shut down debate. "We believe that you have broken covenant." Less than a year later, Rev. Dr. Eklof was dis-fellowshipped.

The actions of UU leadership demonstrate that it is incrementally moving UUism to authoritarianism through an embrace of covenant. Right relations teams ensure conformity. With the posting of a Destructive Behavior policy[82] on the UUA website, there is an intent to push enforcement of accountability down to the congregational level.

In this new world of covenant, we are no longer free to have relationships with one another; we must now have accountable relationships. Consider the mention of accountability in the announcement of the Article II Study Commission. In a recounting of our principles, all but one of our Seven Principles were praised without editorial comment. The only exception is our Fourth Principle, a free and responsible search for truth and meaning. This principle was restated as "**an accountable love in our call for a responsible search for truth and meaning**." (bold added)

The fourth and final observation, to be discussed in more detail shortly, was the lack of historic context regarding our principles provided in the Article II Study Commission announcement. Granted the announcement had much ground to cover and an attempt was made to provide some historical contextual information. It is important that when it comes to revamping the core of UU beliefs, our principles, we are all grounded on a commonly understood foundation of the history of our principles and the factors that resulted in changes.

What is remarkable in the nearly sixty years since our UU principles were first established is that the original intent of our principles has remained consistent despite language changes. However, over the past decade, there has been an effort to frame our principles, sources, and other sections of Article II in more ideological language. The most significant introduction of such ideological language was seen in 2013.

If you feel you have a good understanding of the history of our principles, you can skip down to the section entitled "The Making of our Current Principles and Sources." However, you are encouraged to continue reading.

First Principles

Our first set of Unitarian Universalist principles was established when the Unitarian and Universalist denominations merged in May 1961. Below are the principles as written in Section 2 of Article II of the Constitution at the time of the merger.

> In accordance with these corporate purposes, the members of the Unitarian Universalist Association, dedicated to the principles of a free faith, unite in seeking:
>
> 1. To strengthen one another in a free and disciplined search for truth as the foundation of our religious fellowship;
> 2. To cherish and spread the universal truths taught by the great prophets and teachers of humanity in every age and tradition, immemorially summarized in the Judeo-Christian heritage as love to God and love to man;
> 3. To affirm, defend and promote the supreme worth of every human personality, the dignity of man, and the use of the democratic method in human relationships;
> 4. To implement our vision of one world by striving for a world community founded on ideals of brotherhood, justice and peace;
> 5. To serve the needs of member churches and fellowships, to organize new churches and fellowships, and to extend and strengthen liberal religion;

6. To encourage cooperation with men of good will in every land.[83]

The greatest debate, led by the Universalists, was the lack of emphasis placed on the Judeo-Christian tradition and the absence of wording such as "the truths taught by Jesus." These references were alternately dropped, then added back, and then modified.[84] Although the principles were a faithful representation of the two denominations, they also reflected the compromises required to integrate two denominations that had traveled different liberal religious paths.

Liberal Paths of Unitarianism and Universalism

Both denominations emerged as alternatives to the harsh Calvinist dogma that believed in the depravity of humankind and the predestination of souls. Both Unitarians and Universalists considered themselves Christian. Both were roundly ostracized by orthodox Christians for not being Christian. As noted earlier, the Commission on Institutional Change did a good job summarizing the core beliefs of these faith traditions. Universalism believed that a loving God would never condemn any portion of humanity to eternal damnation. Unitarians had a long tradition of discerning truth based on facts, reason, and investigation. There were, however, distinct characteristics of Universalists and Unitarians that would lead one to believe that they would continue on their separate paths.

Universalism appealed to the "common man," ministers were typically self-taught, members lacked upper socio-economic status by and large and, most importantly, Universalists theologically aligned with a biblical scriptural model. The near opposite could be said of the appeal of Unitarianism to a more educated class with Harvard-graduated ministers serving the elite within society and, most importantly, their theology aligned with rational reasoning.

Unitarians, unlike Universalists, found their theological foundations under constant review and challenge. Shortly after the formation of the American Unitarian Association (AUA) in 1825, Theodore Parker, personifying the transcendentalist movement, challenged Unitarianism with radical views on biblical criticism, theology, and politics. The Transcendentalist movement is mentioned as an example of the state of flux and re-examination that the newly formed denomination faced in its formative years. To address a perceived shortcoming of the American Unitarian Association—that it was merely an association of people and not churches—the National Conference of Unitarian and Other Christian Churches was organized in 1865. The National Conference of Unitarian and Other Christian Churches had a mission to spur denominational activity, but, as the name implied, it adopted a distinctly Christian platform, affirming that its members were "disciples of the Lord Jesus Christ." Three years later, action was taken at its annual meeting to expand the first mission of the American Unitarian Association from "To collect and diffuse information respecting the state of Unitarian Christianity" to read:

> The objective of the American Unitarian Association shall be to diffuse the knowledge and promote the interest of pure Christianity; And all Unitarian Christians shall be invited to Unite and cooperate with it for that purpose.[85]

There was reaction within Unitarianism that opposed what some called the creedal demands of the National Conference. In 1866 the Free Religious Association (FRA) was formed "to encourage the scientific study of theology and to increase fellowship in the spirit." The Western Unitarian Conference (WUC) formed in 1852 to promote Unitarianism west of New York State adopted a position similar to the FRA. By 1875 the WUC was at such odds with the denomination's eastern orthodox Unitarians that the WUC was warned it was slipping dangerously far from Unitarianism's commitment to God and worship. That warning was not without merit. Leaders in the Western Unitarian Conference were integral in the writing of the 1933 Humanist Manifesto. The result of these movements was that Unitarians would gradually disconnect their theology from Christianity, biblical scripture, and theism. However, that "disconnecting" was still decades away. The language adopted regarding the mission of the AUA in the early 1930s would remain largely intact up to 1951.

> In accordance with the charter, the American Unitarian Association shall "be devoted to moral, religious, educational and charitable purposes in accordance with these purposes."

In accordance with these purposes the American Unitarian Association shall:

- Diffuse the knowledge and promote the interests of religion which Jesus taught as love to God and love to man;
- Strengthen the churches and fellowships which unite in the Association for more and better work for the Kingdom of God;
- Organize new churches and fellowships for the extension of Unitarianism in our own country and other lands; and
- Encourage sympathy and cooperation among religious liberals at home and abroad.[86]

Universalists did not experience theological tumult. In 1803 Universalists adopted the Winchester Profession that had even deeper roots from the 1790 Philadelphia Convention of Universalists. The Winchester Profession of Faith remained remarkably stable until the 1961 merger.

Article I. We believe that the Holy Scriptures of the Old and New Testament contain a revelation of the character of God, and of the duty, interest and final destination of mankind.

Article II. We believe that there is one God, whose nature is love, revealed in one Lord Jesus Christ, by one Holy Spirit of Grace, who will finally restore the whole human family of mankind to holiness and happiness.

Article III. We believe that holiness and true happiness are inseparably connected, and their believers ought to be careful to maintain order and practice good work; for these things are good and profitable unto men.

Adding to the stability of the 1803 Winchester Profession of Faith was a clause called the Liberty Clause that was appended to the articles.

> Yet while we adopt a general profession of belief and plan of church government, we leave it to the several churches and societies or to smaller associations of churches, if such should be formed within the limits of our General Association to continue or adopt within themselves such more particular articles of faith or modes of discipline, as may appear to them best under their particular circumstances, provided they do not disagree with our general profession and plan.

That clause recognized the conflict between individual rights and the effort to unify people with diverse beliefs under a single profession of faith. "[W]here the brethren cannot see alike, they may agree to differ."[87] The Liberty Clause remained attached to the Winchester Profession until 1870 and was reinstated in 1899.

In 1933, the same year as the publication of the Humanist Manifesto with 16 of its 34 signatories being current or former Unitarian ministers, the Universalists at their Worcester Convention voted the first approval of an addition to their profession of faith called the Bond of Fellowship. Two years later at the Washington, D.C. Convention, delegates voted 91–0 to adopt this statement that has also become known as the Washington Declaration. The declaration illustrates how

Universalists, who now interpreted their faith as a universalized liberal Christianity, maintained the centrality of Jesus and love.

> The bond of fellowship in this Convention shall be a common purpose to do the will of God as Jesus revealed it and to co-operate in establishing the kingdom for which he lived and died.

> To that end, we avow our faith in God as Eternal and All-conquering Love, in the spiritual leadership of Jesus, in the supreme worth of every human personality, in the authority of truth known or to be known, and in the power of men of good-will and sacrificial spirit to overcome evil and progressively establish the Kingdom of God.[88]

Round Two on the Wording of our Principles

The debate over the language of our principles did not end in 1961. The Universalists, dissatisfied with the lack of emphasis on its scriptural foundation, recommended at the 1962 Washington, D.C., General Assembly, the first after the merger, to entirely replace the language in Section 2, with the following.

> Uniting in the worship of God and the service of man in the promotion of the knowledge and interest of religion as taught by the master prophets of mankind we affirm our faith:
>
> 1. In God, as eternal and all-creative love;
> 2. In the spiritual leadership of Jesus, and the teachings of Buddha, Moses, Muhammed and all the God-men of all the ages;
> 3. In the supreme worth of every human personality;
> 4. In the authority of truth, known and to be known;

5. And in the power of men of goodwill and sacrificial spirit to overcome all evil and progressively establish the Kingdom of God.[89]

This bylaws proposal along with 21 other proposals was considered by the General Assembly with some forwarded to the agenda of the 1963 Chicago General Assembly. One resolution to change the name of the Association to the "Liberal Church of America" was voted down and thus not advanced.

At the 1963 Chicago General Assembly the proposal to replace the 1961 principles with language proposed at the previous Washington, D.C. General Assembly was defeated. Another minor change to the language of the principles was also defeated on a voice vote. There was, however, far greater debate on a bylaw proposal concerning church membership in the Association (Article II, Section 4 of the Constitution). That section specified requirements that churches must satisfy to be a member of the Association, including the need to make a financial contribution, conduct regular religious services, and other criteria. An additional requirement was offered that read "Maintained a policy of admitting persons to membership without discrimination of race, color or national origin." That additional requirement failed to achieve the two-thirds majority vote required for adoption despite attempts to pass the proposal via two separate votes. The principal controversy centered on whether the amendment would conflict with existing constitutional provisions guaranteeing congregational polity in churches and fellowships.[90] The discussion on this matter did not end with the vote.

After disposing of the remaining bylaws proposals, a vigorous debate resumed on this topic that resulted in a resolution designed to advance the spirit of the defeated bylaws proposal. By a vote of 583 to 6 a resolution was passed that read in part:

> WHEREAS, refusal to welcome persons into membership in any of our churches or fellowships because of race, color, or national origin would contradict our historical testimony and the declared constitutional purposes of our Association;
>
> THEREFORE BE IT RESOLVED, that all member congregations of the Unitarian Universalist Association be charged to declare and practice their faith in the dignity and worth of every person and that all member congregations of our denomination are hereby strongly urged to welcome into their membership and full participation persons without regard to race, color, or national origin . . .

The resolution also resulted in the creation of a Commission on Religion and Race that was charged "to promote the complete integration of Negroes and other minority persons into our congregations, denominational life, ministry and into the community."[91]

The debate on the language of our principles and the issue related to race, however, was not over. Two proposals were made at the 1965 Boston General Assembly that continued the debate. One proposal, inspired by the Universalists, was to change the wording in the preamble of Section 2 in Article II, essentially replacing the concept that UUs "[unite] in the worship of God" to "unite in the spirit of Jesus." The second proposal regarding race continued the debate from the year before and targeted the wording in our Third Principle changing the language from:

> To affirm, defend and promote the supreme worth of every human personality, the dignity of man, and the use of the democratic method in human relationships;

to:

> To affirm the supreme worth of every human personality **without regard to race, color or national origin**, to maintain the dignity of man and to promote and defend the use of the democratic method in human relationships; (bold added)

Neither of these proposals to change the preamble or the third principle was adopted. The first proposal was tabled. The second proposal generated a great deal of debate that was now conducted under the heading of "Open Membership Policy." Again, a resolution was issued stating the UUA policy that membership was open to all regardless of race, color, sex (mentioned here for the first time), national origin or creedal test. This time a more permanent solution was put into motion that was finalized at the 1967 Denver General Assembly. At that General Assembly, based on a recommendation of the Committee on Congregational Polity and Membership Practices, a new section, Section 4, was added to Article II that specifically addressed the policy and intention of the UUA to be open and welcoming to all. That section read.

> In accordance with the purposes and objectives of the Unitarian Universalist Association, this Association hereby declares and affirms its special responsibility and the responsibility of its members to promote the full participation of persons, without regard to race, color, sex, or national origin, in the Association, in member churches and fellowships, in associate members, in the ministry and in society.

Over the years this section was updated with wording to reflect the growing list of individuals and communities welcomed into UUism (*e.g.,* disability, affectional or sexual orientation, age, language, citizenship status, economic status).

The Making of our Current Principles and Sources

Aside from a small modification in 1974 to the wording of the 1961 principles replacing male-centric with gender-neutral language (*e.g.,* "man" to "humankind") our original principles remained unchanged for two decades.

In the 1980s a bottom-up initiative resulted in a significant update to our principles. Sponsoring this initiative was the UU Women's Federation (UUWF). The UUWF was formed in 1963 from the merger of two historic women's groups, the Association of Universalist Women, founded in 1869, and the Alliance of Unitarian and Other

Liberal Christian Women, founded in 1890. The UUWF, aware that the U.S. had undergone a cultural shift in the use of language and the understanding of gender roles, advocated for further updates to our principles. A draft of the new principles was available by 1982, and votes were taken in 1984 and 1985 that finalized the process. A revised set of Seven Principles was adopted in 1985 along with the creation of Five Sources.

> We, the member congregations of the Unitarian Universalist Association, covenant to affirm and promote
>
> 1. The inherent worth and dignity of every person;
> 2. Justice, equity and compassion in human relations;
> 3. Acceptance of one another and encouragement to spiritual growth in our congregations;
> 4. A free and responsible search for truth and meaning;
> 5. The right of conscience and the use of the democratic process within our congregations and in society at large;
> 6. The goal of world community with peace, liberty, and justice for all;
> 7. Respect for the interdependent web of all existence of which we are a part.

With the introduction of Sources to augment our Seven Principles, the historic influence of Judeo-Christian teachings as a source for Unitarian Universalism was preserved. The Five Sources also reflected that in the two decades since the merger, our religious diversity had expanded. There were now other traditions, both religious and non-religious, that informed Unitarian Universalism.

1. Direct experience of that transcending mystery and wonder, affirmed in all cultures, which moves us to a renewal of the spirit and an openness to the forces which create and uphold life;
2. Words and deeds of prophetic men and women which challenge us to confront powers and structures of evil with justice, compassion, and the transforming power of love;
3. Wisdom from the world's religions which inspires us in our ethical and spiritual life;
4. Jewish and Christian teachings which call us to respond to God's love by loving our neighbors as ourselves;
5. Humanist teachings which counsel us to heed the guidance of reason and the results of science and warn us against idolatries of the mind and spirit.

A sixth source was added in 1995: spiritual teachings of Earth-centered traditions which celebrate the sacred circle of life and instruct us to live in harmony with the rhythms of nature. At the 2018 Kansas City General Assembly, the wording of the second source was adjusted, replacing "men and women" with "people" to reflect a more refined understanding of gender-neutral language.

Despite these updates, our principles have remained remarkably faithful to the spirit of the principles practiced by our Unitarian and Universalist ancestors. We can see the reflection of the 1961 principles in the 1985 principles.

- A "free and disciplined search for truth" appears in our Fourth Principle, a free and responsible search for truth and meaning.

- "Defend and promote the supreme worth of every human personality" appears in our First Principle, the inherent worth and dignity of every person.
- "The use of the democratic method in human relationships" is upheld in our Fifth Principle, the right of conscience and the use of the democratic process within our congregations and in society at large.
- The aspiration to strive "for a world community founded on ideals of brotherhood, justice and peace" and the encouragement for "cooperation with men of good will in every land" are echoed in our Second Principle, justice, equity and compassion in human relations and our Sixth Principle, the goal of world community with peace, liberty, and justice for all.

Also included in the 1985 revision of our principles was an update to the less-than-compelling purpose for the Association to "exercise its corporate powers for religious, educational and charitable purposes." The new purpose of the Association was more clearly stated as "The primary purpose of the Association is to serve the needs of its member congregations, organize new congregations, extend and strengthen Unitarian Universalist institutions and implement its principles."

2009 Updates to Article II Voted Down

At the 2009 Salt Lake City General Assembly, a vote to advance another revision to Article II to the agenda of the next General Assembly failed. The review of the principles, sources, and other sections of Article II was commissioned by the UUA Board of Trustees in April 2006 when they asked the Commission on Appraisal (COA) to conduct the review.[92] The Commission on Appraisal is a bylaws-defined standing committee of the Association with independent oversight responsibilities to review functions and activities that would benefit the Association. The Article II review was initiated by the board in accordance with Article XV of the Association's bylaws that specifies that a review of Article II must occur at least every 15 years.[93] Rather than forming an Article II Study Commission, the Commission on Appraisal was a logical choice for the assignment. The Commission on Appraisal had recently completed its report, *Engaging Our Theological Diversity*, that explored several aspects about UUs including our relationships with one another and our willingness to continue our path, spiritual or not, through an ongoing search for truth and meaning.

The Commission on Appraisal is to be commended for approaching the review with the gravity and reverence required by such an endeavor. Lacking a creedal statement, profession of faith, or theological requirement, our principles are central to our Unitarian Universalist identity. They are the unifying glue that holds together the widely diverse, eclectic group of people who collectively call themselves Unitarian Universalists.

Equally commendable is the fact that the Commission did good work. The COA made every effort to engage UUs. They developed guiding questions, such as "What values should guide decision-making about whether and how to revise the text of Article II?"[94] They designed a curriculum with the express intent to invoke thoughtful reflection and discussion rather than have people engage in "off-the-cuff" comments. Both an online and print curriculum were developed, allowing congregations to hold one-session or five-session workshops to be engaged in the process. They reached out to lay and professional leadership, identity groups, and youth and adult constituents. They sent out surveys and received 1,700 online responses as well as many comments that filled over 450 pages. All very good and thoughtful work.

We also learned from the work of the Commission on Appraisal that a "review" initiative can quickly morph into an overwhelming compulsion to change. The COA initially anticipated resistance to changes to Article II but ended their work with a considerable number of recommended revisions. Some revisions were trivial and some substantive. The trivial changes involved the wording of the principles. Several words in the principles were dropped to make them easier to memorize. The Fifth Principle, the right of conscience and the use of the democratic process within our congregations and in society at large, for example, saw everything after "process" trimmed away. All Seven Principles and their order were preserved despite comments to reorder the sequence.

The COA approach to our Six Sources was more aggressive. The bulleted list of our sources was eliminated, and a three-paragraph narrative inserted. In typical UU fashion, the COA received a deluge of comments. Some suggested that the reference to Jewish and Christian teachings should be replaced by a simple reference to "all of the world's religions." Others wanted explicit references to more religious traditions such as Buddhism and Islam. Some saw an inference in the ordering of the list. Humanists felt their contribution to UUism was being discounted. In the end, the three-paragraph narrative offered by the Commission on Appraisal had its own faults. We will consider only the first two paragraphs.

The first paragraph attempted to anchor today's UUism on its inheritance from the religious heritages of Unitarianism and Universalism.

> Unitarian Universalism is rooted in two religious heritages. Both are grounded on thousands of years of Jewish and Christian teachings, traditions, and experiences. The Unitarian heritage has affirmed that we need not think alike to love alike and that God is one. The Universalist heritage has preached not hell but hope and courage, and the kindness and love of God. Contemporary Unitarian Universalists have reaped the benefits of a legacy of prophetic words and deeds.

It could be argued that the Unitarian heritage is poorly if not misrepresented. The 2020 Commission on Institutional Change did a better job capturing the essence of the Unitarian heritage, with its reference to a tradition of discerning truth based on facts, reason, and investigation. The reference to the Universalist tradition that preached "not hell but hope" was an awkward reference to an incorrectly attributed quote by Rev. John Murray, "Go out into the highways and by-ways of America, your new country . . . Give them, not hell, but hope and courage," something Rev. Murray never said![95] The standard for the scholarship in Article II must be impeccable and beyond reproach.

The second paragraph invites two criticisms. One, the attempt to list religious traditions by name faced the inevitable question, "Why include that tradition and not this tradition?" The second criticism is the questionable and controversial reference to "liberation theologies." The second paragraph, nonetheless, had a good start:

> Unitarian Universalism is not contained in any single book or creed. Its religious authority lies in the individual, nurtured and tested in the congregation and the wider world.

If the COA had simply stopped here, clarity and completeness would have been achieved. The narrative, unfortunately, continued with a list of religious traditions such as Humanism, earth-centric and Eastern religions and concluded by highlighting the influence of liberation theologies. The inclusion of liberation theologies is problematic due to its linkage back to postmodernism and Critical Race Theory terminology.

Faux Democracy on Display

Although the final version of the Fifth Principle Task Force report would not be produced for another half year, the outlines of the report's conclusions about the failure of General Assembly to be truly representative and the lack of delegate knowledge about the implications of the business being decided were already well known. At the 2009 General Assembly, only a tiny percentage of UUs participated in the decision on new UU principles. Of the denomination's 164,684 members,[96] only 0.7% of UUs were engaged in that decision, the final vote being 573 to 586.[97] This General Assembly also had a marquee vote for a new president of the Association that pre-occupied many delegates. That raises the question of just how much attention was devoted to a decision impacting our principles and sources.

We have only a narrow window into the decision process of one delegate, a first-time delegate who blogged their General Assembly experience.

> The other vote I cast was against the by-law changes, which failed by such a small margin that I practically decided the issue myself. And that is a scary thought, I guess, because I am what the pros call a "single-issue, low-information voter."
>
> Like the guy in the voting line, I had read the revised UU Sources and I didn't like them.[98]

2013 Article II Change - Ghost of 2009

Four years later at the 2013 Louisville General Assembly, two changes to Article II were again offered for initial approval so that they could be advanced for a final vote at the 2014 General Assembly. The first change was to Section C-2.3 known as the Non-discrimination section.

The Non-discrimination section, as we have learned, was added to Article II at the 1967 General Assembly after several years of debate to determine how best to affirm the Association's special responsibility to promote the full participation of people regardless of race, color, etc. As noted earlier in this chapter, the list of communities was expanded over the years. At the 2013 General Assembly, the process was initiated to relocate this Article II Non-discrimination section to the Rules section of the bylaws (G-2.3. Non-discrimination). The procedure for amending a bylaws rule is less onerous than Article II, thus enabling the list of communities covered by the intent of the Non-discrimination language to be more readily updatable. This change appears to be a sound and reasonable amendment.

The second change to Article II was the replacement of the Non-discrimination section with a section called Inclusion. There had been discussions that the use of "inclusive" language was a better way to promote a positive and affirming messaging of UUism openness to all people. "[S]ome of our favorite examples" of inclusive, welcoming language were provided on a UUA website page. One example is provided below.

> Inclusivity and Diversity: The society strives to foster a climate of purposeful inclusion of all people. We value the diversity of racial and cultural identity and background, nationality, sexual and affectional orientation, gender identity and its expression, religious background and belief, marital status, family structure, age, mental and physical health and

ability, political perspective, and educational and class status.[99]

The language adopted in the Association's Article II Inclusion section took, however, a different direction, employing a less welcoming tone. "Systems of power, privilege, and oppression have traditionally created barriers for persons and groups with particular identities, ages, abilities and histories." This language choice, with its Critical Race Theory ideological phraseology, may be a harbinger of what we might expect from the current Article II Study Commission. So how did such wording come to be selected to be included in the same bylaws article where our principles and sources are found?

You will recall at the 2009 Salt Lake City General Assembly, an initial vote to advance changes to Article II for a final vote was defeated. Those changes were drafted by the Commission on Appraisal team as part of their mandate to perform a required 15-year review of Article II. Like the current Article II Study Commission, the Commission on Appraisal took full license "to revise, replace or restructure" all sections in Article II. Among the sections the Commission on Appraisal revised was C-2.3. the Non-discrimination section. It is from the work done by the Commission on Appraisal from 2007-2009 that the language of "systems of power" was first offered for the Inclusion section in Article II. This use of ideological language by the Commission on Appraisal is not unexpected given the findings contained in the Commission's published report *Engaging Our Theological Diversity.* Chapter 7, "New UU Orthodoxy" covers this topic in more detail.

It should be noted that the Commission on Appraisal also made a substantive change to the intent of another section in Article II called Freedom of Belief. The Freedom of Belief statement continues to read in our bylaws as:

> Nothing herein shall be deemed to infringe upon the individual freedom of belief which is inherent in the Universalist and Unitarian heritages or to conflict with any statement of purpose, covenant, or bond of union used by any congregation unless such is used as a creedal test.

The language offered by the Commission on Appraisal at the 2009 General Assembly replaced the concept of "individual freedom" with "congregational freedom."

> Congregational freedom is central to the Unitarian Universalist heritage.
>
> Congregations may establish statements of purpose, covenants, and bonds of union so long as they do not require a statement of belief as a creedal test for membership; nor may the Association employ such a test for congregational affiliation.

Although the changes to Article II presented at the 2009 General Assembly were voted down, a second life was given to the Inclusion section by a responsive resolution that requested the UUA Board of

Trustees to continue to pursue the adoption of the "systems of power" language in the Inclusion section."[100]

Lessons from this Experience

Since the UUA Board both commissions study groups and reviews/approves the output of these study groups, one can see that over the past decade there has been an intent by our UU leadership to reshape UUism by altering the language in Article II. Given the language in the 2020 Commission on Institutional Change report on congregational polity and congregational autonomy, there may be attempts to alter these long-standing pillars in our Association's governance model. Given the sweeping administrative powers of the UUA Board and its control over the agenda of General Assembly, we can see that even after congregational delegates at a General Assembly reject changes to Article II, that vote can be administratively challenged. In the case of the Inclusion section of Article II, those changes were resurrected and brought forward again. With the structural brokenness of our General Assembly to be a truly representative body, will the character of UUism eventually be worn down simply by the persistence of an unresponsive leadership team?

However, if we take a long view from the history of our principles, we can see the norms that should surround the process for modifying our principles, sources, and freedom of belief statement in Article II. The process must be respectful of the heritage intent of our principles and the complex, maybe even cumbersome, decisioning structure to alter our principles. Our principles belong to all UUs and keeping them free of the dogma or ideology of a particular group is a triumph for all UUs.

Another important lesson is that congregational polity is to be as deeply valued as our principles. This observation is particularly germane given that our UU leadership has thrown the bureaucratic power of the Association and its assumed ecclesiastical power behind a revision of our principles. It does not appear that our Boston-based leaders value the independence and autonomy of congregations. These concepts of independence and autonomy, like our principles, reflect our religious heritages, were enshrined in our denomination's original constitution, and continue to be supported in our current bylaws. Changes to our bylaws should be a holistic effort, not a single-minded focus to impose a narrow interpretation of our core UU beliefs.

Lastly, reflecting on the failure to advance their efforts on Article II in 2009, the Commission on Appraisal conceded that unlike in 1985, they did not have grassroots support. "There was only the Bylaw section mandating review every fifteen years."

Since we are headed for another vote on bylaws changes to Article II in 2022, we should all become aware of the scope and impact of these bylaws changes. Admittedly, getting excited about bylaws changes has all the appeal of eating dry desert sand, but upcoming bylaws changes will impact our principles and sources and most likely our guarantee of congregational polity, autonomy, and independence.

Let us not allow our principles to slip away simply for a lack of attention. It is important that all UUs read everything from the Article II Study Commission, no matter how dry the sand.

6.   What a Difference One Year Makes

In 2016 the Unitarian Universalist Association published its *UU World* Seeker #1 edition. Christopher L. Walton, the magazine's editor, shared in his Welcome comments that this special edition of *UU World* was designed as an "introduction to the distinctive liberal religion known as Unitarian Universalism." Walton continued, "If you're just getting acquainted with Unitarian Universalism, I hope these stories and images give you a useful glimpse into our spiritually curious, community minded, intellectually restless and justice-oriented faith community."

As a historian (co-author Jay), it is valuable to find an issue of a periodical with a snapshot in time with a self-assessment of our religious movement.   These snapshots freeze for a moment religious debate, controversy, or celebration and provide an anchor point to my research. I can then explore "we were here at this point in time" and ask, "Did we stay the course or alter our trajectory?"

I have read many such articles in bygone periodicals such as Thomas Whittemore's *Trumpet and Universalist Magazine,* John Burruss' *Universalist Herald* and the Unitarians' *The Christian Register* that merged with *The Universalist Leader* in 1961 and eventually published under the name of *UU World*. What emerges from this reading is a consistency across generations of editors and writers. The phrasing used by the *UU World* editor, Chris Walton, regarding "our spiritually curious, community minded, intellectually restless and justice-oriented faith community" would not have seemed out of place by any of his heritage predecessors. This 2016 Seeker issue also serves as an official view of how Unitarian Universalism saw itself just one year before the rather abrupt declaration that the denomination was based on white supremacy culture, was racist and oppressive.

Who We Are

The first of ten articles in the Seeker Edition, entitled "Who We Are," was penned by Melissa Harris-Perry who at the time was the Maya Angelou Presidential Chair at Wake Forest University. Some may know Harris-Perry from her time as a host and commentator on the cable network MSNBC. Speaking in a first-person voice, Harris-Perry observed that UUism was not tied to any dogma, but rather was committed to "striking a balance between the openness to the differing viewpoints on one hand and the fierce advocacy of shared ethical claims on the other."[101] Near the end of her article, Harris-Perry makes an assertion that may be the roadmap to UU health and unity. "Our faith is a belief that we can embrace the common good through how we interact with one another by holding fast to our precepts of inclusion, participation and non-judgmental disagreement."[102] If only we could find once again that spirit of non-judgmental behavior.

What We Believe

In another article entitled "What We Believe," Rev. Dr. Galen Guengerich, then Senior Minister of All Souls Church in New York City, observed, "Over the past 500 years or so, human beings have come to rely more and more on reason and science as the basis for human knowledge." Those last "500 years or so" correspond to the period known as the Enlightenment. Guengerich continued by stating that there has been a long religious argument between those who claim revelation as the source of truth versus those who hold that one need not suspend reason when seeking truth. Guengerich closed the argument by stating that for UUs, "reason trumps revelation every time."[103]

Meet the Love People

The article "Meet the 'Love People'" by Chris Walton spoke to the public engagement of UUism that before the inward turn taken by our current UU leadership, felt like the natural extension of UUism's social justice DNA. The article recounted the 2010 event when hundreds of UUs, wearing their distinctively yellow Standing on the Side of Love t-shirts, protested Arizona's anti-illegal immigrant law, S.B. 1070, also known as the "your papers, please" law, that made it a state crime for any non-citizen who could not produce their alien registration certificate. The story highlighted the power of the denomination's public symbolism, its yellow shirts. The UU front person charged with introducing President Peter Morales to the local and national press

107

found the standard introduction, "Would you like to speak to the President of the Unitarian Universalist Association?" was simply not getting traction. But "Would you like to talk to the leader of the yellow shirts?" invoked an immediate response of "yes."

The Standing on the Side of Love campaign was initiated in 2008 following the tragic shooting death of two people at the Tennessee Valley UU Church in Knoxville, Tennessee. The UUA bought a full-page ad in the *New York Times* reading, "We will not give in to fear. We will meet hatred with love." Though maybe the most applicable language from the article that could help us navigate a denomination dividing along the lines of "centered" and "decentered" are the words of Rev. Morales, "We suffer *with*, not separated *from* the other. That's a deeply spiritual experience."[104]

We Have Drifted So Far

It appears that today, we have drifted so very far from what we once considered UUism. Reason and logic are now deemed tools of white supremacy and are thus shunned. Judgmental behavior is now an official UU policy. We have receded from the public square to argue inwardly on the nature of our principles, sources, local autonomy, and congregational polity. I recall a discussion in which I participated that asked the question, "If your congregation suddenly disappeared, what do you think would be the consequences to the wider world?" I extend that question and ask, "If the UUA suddenly disappeared?" I fear no one in the wider world would notice.

Theology

7.   New UU Orthodoxy

Prologue of the Author

The impact of this chapter will be directly proportional to your faith in Unitarian Universalism. What that means is, if you are attending a UU congregation because you seek a refuge from the demands of a previous faith tradition or for the choir or for social groups and casual environment, the concerns addressed in this chapter may not be relevant to you. If on the other hand, you are a UU for deeper reasons that even you may not altogether be able to understand, then hopefully you will find this effort rewarding. I (co-author Frank) say this because I did not really know myself the depth of my UU faith until I started to defend it against the drift of the UU leadership, and defending this liberal faith is to me what this book is all about. What this means will, I hope, be made clear in what follows.

UUism is becoming unrecognizable. Its theological foundation based on our Seven Principles (See Appendix A) is being replaced by an alternate belief system called "liberatory theology." As described in the 2020 report of the Commission on Institutional Change (COIC), this new UU liberatory theology is intended to free Unitarian Universalism from its alleged complicity with white supremacy culture. As discussed in the History section of this book, a handful of UUA Board of Trustee members in 2017 simply declared that UUism was based on white supremacy culture. That declaration put into motion events that have allowed liberatory theology to find a foothold in UUism.

White supremacy is an evocative term laden with strong negative connotations. It is generally acknowledged that white supremacy involves an element in our society that is devoted to the doctrine, be it biological, cultural, or religious, of the inherent superiority of white people over people of color. We have ample examples of organizations that are truly complicit with and advocate white supremacy, such as the Ku Klux Klan, Skinheads, and neo-Nazis. These organizations are what is called the alt-right.

This common understanding of white supremacy was not, however, what UU leadership meant in its 2017 declaration of UUism as complicity in white supremacy. Our UU leadership has been either clumsy or coy in its use of the term white supremacy. They never actually define it, either in their 2017 declaration or in the 2020 COIC report, even though the latter was charged to "analyze structural racism and white supremacy" within our faith community. They even failed to define it when they counseled in the October 2020 UUA Board of Trustees orientation packet to be "mindful to avoid white supremacy behavior," such as urgency and perfectionism. These behaviors were taken from a list developed by Tema Okun and her colleague Kenneth Jones in their work at ChangeWork.[105] The list has no basis in research or scholarship. So, what specifically does our UU leadership mean when they refer to white supremacy?

It has taken a fair amount of research and analysis, but our conclusion is that UU leadership defines white supremacy as a socio-political economic system of domination based on racial categories that benefit those defined and perceived as white. This system rests on the historical and current accumulation of structural power that gives privilege to white people as a group. Unitarian Universalism is, according to this view, a culture mired in power structures that favor whiteness and subjugates people of color. More than that, according to this view, the power structure of UUism overtly oppresses a whole array of people distributed along the intersectionality scale, an idea that emerged from an academic discipline known as critical studies. The intersectionality scale measures the level of oppression a person suffers in society by their membership in one or more identity groups, often overlapping, formed by factors such as race, gender, sex, sexuality, class, ability, nationality, citizenship, religion, and body type.

So just how did UUism, which has been in the vanguard over decades in confronting racism and oppression, become oppressive? Our principles were forged in opposition to racism and oppression. Do we not hold to the worth and dignity of every person? Do we not affirm the right of conscience and the democratic process? Do we not believe in justice, equity, and compassion in all human relations? The answer, of course, is yes. But as I hope to explain, something has changed in the ideological thinking of our UU leadership. Our principles are now seen as obstacles in this newly revised confrontation with racism and oppression and must be "decentered," to use the language of this new liberatory theology. Under the guise of creating what UU leadership calls a "beloved community," UUism is being incrementally altered through a liberatory theology that aims to reshape our faith tradition more in the image of an orthodox autocratic religious institution. The assertion by the Commission of Institutional Change that it is authorized to act under a theological mandate is not accidental. A theological mandate requires conformance and accountability. For the first time in the nearly 50 years that I have been a UU, there are now serious consequences simply for principled dissent. This book is a sincere effort to alert UUs to these dramatic changes and to raise the question: What is happening to our faith and is it something we want to support?

At the Fifth Principle Project, we believe that this new liberatory theology is a tectonic shift from our liberal religious tradition and is happening beneath the radar of most Unitarian Universalists. It behooves all UU's, therefore, to know something about where this is coming from and what it means for the liberal values of UUism. How is it that a faith having social justice baked into the very heart of its meaning finds itself under such a sweeping indictment of white supremacy from its own leadership? UUs value social justice, do we not? What happened to the idea that the way to social justice was not to evaluate people based on race, gender, or sexuality? Should our faith community be listening more actively to minority voices? Absolutely. No true UU would deny it. But should we abandon the liberal tradition that created the very institutions which made such listening both possible and even required? That, as we shall see, is a very real question that emerges from the kind of thinking that currently prevails among UU leadership. Where did this systematic assault on UU liberalism come from and what does it mean for our liberal religious tradition?

Pedigree of Liberatory Theology: Postmodernism

There are sufficient clues both in the 2020 General Assembly program and in the Commission on Institutional Change report that the new liberatory theology would not exist but for the combined impact of at least three critical theories: Postcolonial, Critical Race, and Intersectional Theory. What critical theories are and how they originated is a complex topic that cannot be fully described in this book. We do not, however, need to be experts in the field to get a fair grasp of what they are, where they came from, and that they are being used against UU liberalism. To be clear, this chapter is not about the virtues and vices of postmodernism. Nor it is about the virtues and vices of the various critical theories it spawned. Rather, we seek to describe how this body of thought has been exploited by UU leadership in the development of a liberatory theology that is being deployed in opposition to our liberal religious heritage.

Critical Theory has a deep and enduring history in philosophy. Critical Theory has changed over time and as indicated, there is more than one kind, but we do not have to cover it all here. We just need to concern ourselves with the critical theories that emerged from a body of thought known as postmodernism.

Postmodernism is a school of thought that rejects the liberal values that UUism inherited from Enlightenment modernity. That is what the prefix "post" means in postmodernism. All the critical theories that emerged from postmodernism share their rejection of Enlightenment modernity but in different ways. Each attacks and undermines how we think about knowledge and language in our liberal theological tradition. As we shall see, for the kind of postmodernism prevailing among UU leadership, there is but one primary social and political reality; oppression, spawned by the unequal distribution of power. The source of this oppressive power is none other than the liberal Enlightenment values that birthed UUism.

The Two Waves of Postmodernism

Postmodernism has had two careers.[106] The first emergence of postmodernist thinking swept academia during the 1960s. However, by the 1980s this first wave of postmodernism burned out, primarily due to the ever-increasing convolution of its deconstructionist thinking. A second wave of postmodernism emerged in the 1990s from the embers of its predecessor, expanding into elite universities and eventually finding its way into our UU seminaries. This second wave has been described by Helen Pluckrose, a liberal humanist, author, and editor-in-chief of *Areo*, as "applied postmodernism."[107] This description is important for UUs because the applied version of postmodernism has been embraced by our UU seminaries and is the primary source of the critical theories that have been embraced by UU leadership.

Postmodernism: First Wave

Postmodernism was born in the wake of two world wars and the Great Depression. It was a time when many thinkers experienced a crisis of thought and meaning that resulted in a radical skepticism about the ability of language to grasp and convey any knowledge at all about what the world is really like. This issue is as old as philosophy itself, but this radical skepticism was primarily responsible for the view that humans do not have access to any reality that could be called true. This presented a serious problem, and not just for Unitarian Universalists.

For the Enlightenment tradition, objective reality exists, and human beings have access to it, albeit imperfectly, by using the tools of reason and science as expressed in language. Language, while occasionally slippery, is generally reliable. It is how we communicate and advance knowledge. The more ideas get debated and discussed, the better the approximation to reality and the truth of things. Upon this edifice of a knowable reality rests objective truth accessible through language.

In postmodernism, all of this implodes. In postmodernism, there is no reality. There is no truth. There is only language.

> Direct access to reality, in other words, is impossible, because every phenomenon is thoroughly mediated by language use . . . Nothing avoids the influence of interpretation, and thus reality should be viewed as simply a linguistic invention. Fact, truth, and so forth can only be approached through the nuances of speech.[108]

This view is due to postmodernism's development of the critical method called deconstructionism. It is a method shared by all the critical theories that emerged from postmodernism. Deconstructionism can be very obscure, but it basically holds that language, especially concepts such as truth and justice, is irreducibly complex, unstable, or impossible to determine. The important point for our purposes is that deconstructionism makes it impossible to talk about the world in terms of ideas or any system of ideas that provide overarching accounts, interpretations, or explanations of events. Such explanations provide a structure for our beliefs, giving meaning to our experiences and legitimizing our social and political institutions. Examples of overarching interpretations include Christianity and Marxism, but also the core ideas of the liberal heritage that gave us our Seven Principles, ideas like history, law, nature, progress, reason, science, tradition, and humanity.[109] Perhaps you can begin to see the problem that deconstructionism presents. If there is no reality upon which our ideas are based, if no system of explanation has any real legitimacy, then what does that tell us about the status of all the social and political institutions which are based on them? The answer is, it all disappears into the deconstructive vapor, like the grin of the Cheshire cat.

However, we still have social institutions, because within postmodernism, while language fails to convey or is a barrier to the real world, language does construct our social realities. Postmodernism calls these social realities discourses, or stories, and they are no more than simply ways of talking about things that get taken for knowledge. When postmodernists talk about knowledge as "socially constructed," this is basically what they mean.

> The postmodern world view operates with a community-based understanding of truth. It affirms that whatever we accept as truth and even the way we envision truth are dependent upon the community in which we participate.[110]

We do not, therefore, have knowledge so much as linguistically constructed "ways of knowing," each a bid to impose some form of social order peculiar to some given community; with no basis upon which to evaluate one way of knowing over another. It should be understood by UUs that this "community-based understanding of truth" is the intellectual background for the data gathering method used by the Commission on Institutional Change. The COIC used the stories of marginalized members of our faith to establish the alleged prevalence of white supremacy within Unitarian Universalism (This is extensively addressed in Chapter 3, "Widening the Circle of Concern").

What was left in the wake of this first wave was an unrelieved and unrelievable moral and political relativism. If there is no reality against which to check the veracity of our various interpretations, our stories, then what legitimate avenues are there for giving one more or less value over another? What grounds are there for choosing among ways of life, of judging from good, better and best forms of social order? How can we ascertain or measure social progress?

> For postmodernists, any meaningful critique of a culture's values and ethics from within a different culture is impossible, since each culture operates under different concepts of knowledge and speaks only from its own biases.[111]

The question then of what constitutes legitimate political and social order is left essentially unanswerable. Within postmodernism, there is no legitimate way to talk about the "arc of the moral universe" or to "speak truth to power" because there is no truth, no way to judge good, better and best. Additionally, and more ominously, this has the further and unpleasant implication that any order, whether conceptual or social, can only be achieved by deception or force.[112]

According to some scholars, this relativism is the primary reason postmodernism fell out of fashion in academia in the early 1980s. Its deconstructive method was exceedingly effective at undermining systems of ideas but ended up without resources for creating alternatives to them. Its relativism was so thorough it undermined itself.

It is not possible, on postmodern premises, either for a group to agree on a common platform, or, supposing they could do so, to know whether they are succeeding in carrying out that program in practice. The effect of postmodern rhetoric is to unsettle all institutions and practices without distinction, including those that protect deviants from the wrath of the majority, and at the same time to cut the heart out of any possibility that the resulting confusions could be resolved in a progressive, or even a coherent, way.[113]

Postmodernism: Second Wave

In the end it, was just too deconstructive, and by the mid-1980s postmodern writing began to decline. While it declined in academic circles, it continued to have an enduring impact in two fundamental ways. One, by entering the popular culture in terms of what is known by some scholars as the age of "post-truth"[114] and two, through a revival in academia within various parts of the humanities that look at social justice issues. This is the "applied" version of postmodernism that gave us Postcolonial, Critical Race, and Intersectional theories, all of which were in abundant evidence at the 2020 UU General Assembly and in the report from the Commission on Institutional Change.

All the critical theories that emerged in the second academic wave of applied postmodernism accepted their predecessors' teaching that there is no objective reality, that there are only linguistically constructed social realities. However, applied postmodernists added something that their predecessors denied to themselves. They added an objective reality that they discovered to be right in the midst of all the human social constructions. They developed the view that some of the discourses that construct our social reality, our knowledge(s), become dominant, and because they become dominant, they oppress other ways of knowing. Applied postmodernists, thus, asserted oppression itself as objectively real.[115] This was the one idea the new postmodernists say their old white guy predecessors failed to grasp, largely because deconstruction left them wholly incapable of seeing any reality at all and because they could not see beyond their own privilege.[116] The assertion of oppression as objectively real also provides applied postmodernism with two concepts its predecessor lacked: a political principle and a moral imperative.[117]

A Political Principle

The political principle is that society is formed of systems of power and hierarchies, which decide through dominating discourses what can be known and how. Pluckrose observes about applied postmodernism that "[p]eople are born as blank slates into a system of discourses and positioned by their race, gender, class, and sexuality within systems of power."[118] Some discourse dominates and gets broadly accepted as knowledge in general. This domination of a discourse is not the result of any competition where the dominant discourse is judged to be the best. The discourse that dominates does so because it serves the interests of the powerful. The powerful group in applied postmodernism is straight white men, who for their own interests oppress the understandings and "ways of knowing" of marginalized groups. This bifurcation of human life along the line that distinguishes the oppressed from the oppressor, each living in a fundamentally different world with irreconcilable understandings of reality, is echoed in the Commission on Institutional Change report. The report states pointedly that the "oppressive practices that center the white, straight, cisgender, affluent, abled-body, neurotypical, college-educated experience will make religious community untenable for others."[119] The report further states.

> When we talk about governance, we are talking about power. When we talk about power combined with prejudice and the centering of the dominant group and their ways of being and doing, we are talking about oppression.[120]

A Moral Imperative

The moral imperative that follows is to seek justice for marginalized ways of knowing believed to belong to oppressed groups. Given that society is constituted, according to this theory, only of hierarchies of unequal power distribution, it is incumbent upon us to continually reveal these systems of oppression and work to change them. As Pluckrose writes.

> Thus, while the original postmodern theorists were fairly aimless, using irony and playfulness to reverse hierarchies and disrupt what they saw as unjust power and knowledge (or power-knowledge) structures, the second wave of (applied)

postmodernists focused on dismantling hierarchies and making truth claims about power, language, and oppression. During its applied turn, Theory underwent a moral *mutation* (italics in the original); it adopted a number of beliefs about the rights and wrongs of power and privilege . . . They explicitly stated they were doing this with the purpose of remaking society according to their moral vision—all the while citing the original postmodern Theorists.[121]

If there is one overriding theme in the COIC report, it is the moral reform of Unitarian Universalism, the need to rescue a faith grounded in the liberal heritage of our Seven Principles from its alleged saturation in white supremacist systems of oppression. There is, moreover, another important observation to be noted about the moral crusade of this ideology. Since it is the nature of society to be constituted of unjust power hierarchies, then can the inference be drawn that the struggle against oppression never ends? We believe this is true of this ideology, and on this basis alone, it is difficult to imagine what social justice might look like.

Postcolonial and Critical Race Theories

In the applied postmodernism prevalent among UU leadership, the dominant discourse that everyone is born into and unthinkingly accepts is that of our liberal Enlightenment heritage. The discourse of Enlightenment modernity serves the interests of straight white men, creating inequality. Justice can come only at the price of the Enlightenment modernity that creates the injustice. In Postcolonial theory, this white way of knowing must be "decolonized," which is the postcolonial word for deconstructed. Describing this mindset Pluckrose and Lindsay[122] say postcolonialism holds that the West constructed the idea of rationality and science to perpetuate its own power and marginalize nonrational, nonscientific forms of knowledge from elsewhere. We must now "devalue white, Western ways of knowing" belonging to white Westerners and promote alternative ones "in order to equalize the power balance."[123]

Critical Race Theory has echoed this approach with the same heavy emphasis on the social construction of knowledge, alternative ways of knowing and the "devaluing" of our "white" Enlightenment heritage. As Pluckrose writes, "Critical Race theory holds that race is a social construct that was created to maintain white privilege and white supremacy."[124] Our UU leadership reveals that it actually holds a more strident view of Critical Race Theory than expressed by Pluckrose. In an essay published in the Winter 2018 edition of *UU World*, the official voice of the UUA, Crystal Fleming, an associate professor of sociology and Africana studies at Stony Brook University wrote.

> From a critical race perspective, the United States is not (and never was) a benevolent "nation of immigrants." Rather, it is a nation of settler-colonialism, genocide, white nationalism, racial slavery, legal torture, and institutionalized rape.[125]

Although Crystal Fleming was writing from a sociological viewpoint, Critical Race Theory (CRT) did not have its origin in sociology, but in law. CRT emerged from what is known as Critical Legal Studies (CLS) and spread from there to other academic disciplines. As Khiara M. Bridges, professor of law at UC Berkeley School of Law wrote.

> The adherents of CLS, - or crits, as they came to be called – were a largely white, predominantly male "collection of neo-Marxist intellectuals, former New Left activists, ex-counter culturalists, and other varieties of oppositionists in law schools." What united them was an interest in exposing the law's role in creating, sustaining, and naturalizing a society that they believed to be woefully oppressive and alienating.[126]

The crits, as Bridges goes on to say, developed the deconstructive techniques used by all the critical theories that emerged from postmodernism, but they preferred to focus on the hierarchy and subordination of class rather than race. "CRT ought to be understood as a reaction to CLS's perceived bankruptcy in this regard," writes Bridges."[127] The crits were focused on destabilizing the authority of the law as understood by liberal jurisprudence because they viewed it as nothing more than a "technique of alienation" and a tool for maintaining the hegemonic dominance of the powerful. While this approach was attractive to the advocates of CRT, it was also true that the scholars of color in that emerging discipline knew through the Civil Rights movement that the law could work on behalf of the subjugated. "In their view, the law had done powerful things for the vulnerable."[128]

This impasse led to the development of Critical Race Theory as an independent mode of legal analysis within the field of law.

According to Bridges, Critical Race Theory developed a complicated and somewhat contradictory way of thinking about the law. On the one hand, the advocates of CRT agreed with the crits that the law was a tool of oppression, while on the other they recognized the emancipatory potential the law possesses. That is to say, they saw their work as a continuation of the Civil Rights movement while holding that liberal values of neutral principles of law are insufficient to address the persistent problem of racism. In short, they had their proverbial feet in both modernism and postmodernism.

Critical Race Theory subsequently expanded out of legal studies into other disciplines concerned with social justice, notably sociology, history, political science, economics, and education. Among these disciplines, the understanding of Critical Race Theory tends to be more in line with that of Kimberlé Crenshaw, a founder of Critical Race Theory and the progenitor of the concept of intersectionality. Crenshaw combined Critical Race Theory with Feminism, adding gender justice to that of racial justice, expanding the levels and combinations of identity politics.

> Furthermore, this Theoretical approach allowed for evermore categories of marginalized identity to be incorporated into the intersectional analysis, adding layer upon layer of apparent sophistication and

complexity to the concept, and the scholarship and activism that utilizes it.[129]

These CRT practitioners view liberal values as having no enduring basis in principle and see them as mere social constructs calculated to protect and advance the interests of the dominant group—straight white men. The important point for Unitarian Universalists is the common opposition among Critical Race and Postcolonial theorists to our Enlightenment liberal order. Two prominent proponents of Critical Race Theory, Richard Delgado and Jean Stenic, observed that these social justice advocates have abandoned our liberal tradition.

> The critical race theory (CRT) movement is a collection of activists and scholars engaged in studying and transforming the relationship among race, racism, and power. The movement considers many of the same issues that conventional civil rights and ethnic studies discourses take up but places them in a broader perspective that includes economics, history, setting, group and self-interest, and emotions and the unconscious.
>
> Unlike traditional civil rights discourse, which stresses incrementalism and step-by-step progress, **critical race theory questions the very foundations of the liberal order**, including equality theory, legal reasoning, Enlightenment rationalism, and neutral principles of constitutional law.[130] (bold added)

Without the liberal order inherited from Enlightenment modernity, there could be no Unitarian Universalism and no Seven Principles. The implication here is that if one questions "the very foundations of the liberal order," then one questions the very foundations of Unitarian Universalism. We at the Fifth Principle Project believe that this is what UU leadership is doing.

This applied postmodernist strain of Critical Race Theory with its skepticism toward our liberal heritage is now in ascendancy among UU leadership. It is not surprising then, that in the battle regarding white supremacy, oppression, and persistent problems of race, gender or any other form of social injustice, the liberal order is viewed either as inadequate or as itself the source of oppression. In this context, it is even more alarming to see UU leadership now claiming a theological mandate as a source of governing authority and rationale for substantial changes to our principles.

The Influence of Applied Postmodernism

Postcolonial Theory

The entire 2020 General Assembly program was steeped in applied postmodern oppression as advanced in Postcolonial Theory. Despite a valiant effort to convey the laudable message that UUism will strive to lift up minority and historically marginalized voices, the entire program was overwhelmed by a strident sense of grievance and retribution and a sweeping indictment of Enlightenment modernity and our legacy of UU liberalism as having wrought nothing but oppression and genocide. From the keynote address and the Action of Immediate Witness (AIW) declarations to presentations like "Settler Colonialism and a History of Erasure and Exclusion," and "Settler Colonialism and

Genocide," the entire structure and content of the General Assembly program was based on Postcolonial Theory. Echoing, again and again, the view of the opening speech by Roxanne Dunbar-Ortiz, that we should be mourning, not celebrating, the 400-year anniversary of the Mayflower's arrival in 1620.

Roxanne Dunbar-Ortiz's opening speech set the tone for the event. Taken from her book, *Settler Colonialism, White Supremacy, and a History of Erasure and Exclusion*, Dunbar-Ortiz purported to show how the United States had its origins not so much in the Declaration of Independence, but more in what she called the imperialist and genocidal "Doctrine of Discovery" that was declared by European monarchies during the 15th century to legitimize the colonization of lands outside of Europe. It was presented by Dunbar-Oritz as little more than a license to murder Indigenous people.

After saying that the United States rarely mentions this doctrine in historical or even legal texts, she then proceeded to portray the U.S. as rationalizing colonial dominion over the Indigenous with white nationalist ideology that is allegedly embedded in the Constitution. This white nationalism is further protected and reproduced by the pervasive myth that the U.S. is a "nation of immigrants." It is on this basis that she castigates Lin-Manuel Miranda for obfuscating or even perverting this history with his Broadway hit *Hamilton*. Miranda, she says, was born and grew up in New York in a wealthy Puerto Rican family, but presents himself as an immigrant while identifying with Alexander

Hamilton, the creator of American capitalism. She goes on to disparage the casting of hip hop, black and Puerto Rican actors playing white founding fathers, most of whom were slave owners or speculators in the slave trade, as something of a cruel joke that "we need to think deeply about."

Combined with other programs following her speech, particularly the AIW-A "Addressing 400 Years of White Supremacist Colonialism," almost the entire program concerned itself with the history of oppression in the U.S. It sought to depict the liberal legacy of a free church giving birth to democracy as itself a cover for the subjugation and murder of Indigenous people. Consider this "whereas" clause from among the many in the AIW-A that passed by an overwhelming vote of General Assembly delegates.

> WHEREAS, many Unitarian Universalist congregations uncritically trace their origins to the Pilgrims' "Free Church" tradition – a mythos that sanctifies white supremacy and depends upon erasure of Indigenous peoples.[31]

The free church tradition is established in congregational polity. In that tradition, a free church is a democratic institution in the sense that it is intrinsically separate from government (as opposed to a theocracy, or an "established" state church). A free church does not define government policy, and a free church does not accept church theology or policy definitions from the government. In the AIW adopted at General Assembly, however, a free church in that tradition is little more than a church that sanctifies white supremacy and the erasure of Indigenous peoples.

Additionally, this "whereas" clause has an important footnote attached that smears the entire history of the contribution our faith tradition has made to the development of democratic institutions.

> Unitarian Universalist history often miscredits the "covenant communities" of the Pilgrims with bringing democracy and the "Free Church" to the North American continent – and with planting these values within UU tradition. This telling of UU history denies Indigenous histories, cultures, spiritual traditions, and rights.

This is a transparent suggestion that our history as related through our religious liberal tradition of democracy and rights is little more than a fraudulent cover for denying and suppressing the histories, the "knowledges" and denying the rights of other cultures and traditions.

Critical Race Theory

The strong influence of Postcolonial Theory on the 2020 General Assembly was matched by the influence of Critical Race Theory in what was arguably the centerpiece of the whole program, the report of the UUA Board's Commission on Institutional Change (COIC), in which this dim view of our history is echoed. We know that Critical Race Theory is involved because in the wake of the publication of the COIC report, Dr. Elias Ortega, a commission member and esteemed President of Meadville Lombard Theological School in Chicago, felt the need to use Facebook to present a full-throated embrace of Critical Race theory and a defense of using it to write the COIC report.

> The UUA-GA 2020 Season is in full swing. With the release of the Commission on Institutional Change report, "Widening the Circle of Concern," I imagine that some folks will be reading it looking for flaws to dismiss it from the outset. I imagine this will happen primarily because the report mobilizes aspects of **Critical Race Theory** to engage the impact of structural racism.[32] (bold added)

Ortega continued, "Although I could be wrong, I imagine that many within the wing of our movement cemented in classical liberalism as their political outlook will take exception to the use of Critical Race Theory in the report."[33] He adds that those cemented in classical liberalism may also be invested in "in incrementalist politics as their preferred option for social change." This is noteworthy because Dr. Ortega appears to be following Richard Delgado and Jean Stefanic, who hold that incrementalist politics is characteristic of traditional civil rights discourse, which in turn is rooted in the liberal order abandoned by Critical Race Theory.

For those unfamiliar with the vagaries of postmodernism, Critical Race Theory and other related ideologies and what they might mean for UUism, Dr. Ortega suggests that we need not be concerned. In the third paragraph of his Facebook defense of CRT, he takes pains to tell readers that if they want to comment on such matters, they need to have done the requisite work required to understand the subtleties of Critical Race Theory, as he says he has. The implication seems to be that this is likely too complicated for the average UU to grasp, so it is best left to leadership.

Language Is Dangerous

In our view, UU leadership has offered an interpretation of our history as a country, and of our liberal faith as part of that history, as having been little more than the story of avaricious and murderous white people protecting and advancing the interests of white supremacy. This is the primary reason we believe that in the end, all the changes being urged in the COIC report intended to demolish white supremacy culture spell the destruction of UU religious liberalism as well.

We believe there is something else critically important that needs to be addressed. In the applied version of postmodernism prevalent among UU leadership, the purpose of language in discourses is to convey power and construct what passes for knowledge. Recall that from this perspective power oppresses. The dominant discourse is taken for knowledge and oppresses marginalized forms of discourse. In this view, therefore, language has become dangerous in a way it has not been since pre-modern times and needs to be controlled.

The drive of this ideology to control language has been a major concern for many who have written about the identity politics, safetyism, and political correctness of applied postmodernism.[134] This involves the avoidance, sometimes taken to the extreme, of forms of expression in the dominant discourse that is perceived to harm marginalized groups of people. UU leadership is no different. We believe this is among the reasons that the subject of harm and the prevention of it is so dominant in the COIC report. The subject of harm is mentioned 49 times, the first time on the first page just under the copyright notice, where reprint permission for *Stopping Harm, Restoring Relationship, Responding to Microaggression and Oppression* from the Fahs Collaborative of Meadville Lombard is acknowledged.[135] This is the rationale for the effort leadership is investing toward managing our speech through the increasing emphasis being placed on accountability through covenants.

UU Liberalism as a Source of Oppression

Our UU faith was birthed in and is deeply beholden to our Enlightenment heritage with its support for equality, democracy, individual rights, reason, and science. This legacy is now regarded as the source of the dominant discourse. It may be easy to understand at this point why, when the COIC was commissioned by the UUA Board in 2017, the report focused so much on power, the "power structure" and the "power mapping" within Unitarian Universalism.[22] From our perspective, it is because UU leadership, under the influence of applied postmodernism, is now behaving as though the liberal core of our faith is not just "a" source of oppression, but "*the*" source of oppression. This may sound hyperbolic to some, but UU leadership had already been moving solidly in this direction. In 2005, before the days when the UU leadership started to talk in terms of white supremacy culture, its own Commission on Appraisal made what can only be described as a full-throated embrace of the applied postmodern approach to the Enlightenment heritage at the core of our faith. From its 2005 report *Engaging Our Theological Diversity*, the commission made it sound as though our commitment to Enlightenment modernity was probably an historic mistake. Under the section entitled "Outgrowing the Enlightenment Worldview," it states.

> Unitarianism in particular claims strong roots in the Enlightenment. Its gifts are enduring; reason—a valuing of evidence and the scientific method; tolerance—the possibility of valuing multiple perspectives; and freedom—an appreciation of introspection, autonomy, and individual vs. role identity (which prepared the ground for such movements as women's suffrage).
>
> The Enlightenment moved humans out of the center of the universe and encouraged imaginative possibility. Now we need to ask ourselves if it is possible that we have identified too strongly with a particular worldview and philosophical era. Could a continuing evolution of worldviews leave UUs holding the rear guard instead of the front lines at this time in history?[136]

In other words, since some are questioning their faith in Enlightenment modernity, why should UU's be any different? The report then devoted subsequent pages to justifying why we should follow, or even lead, the rest of the world in its rejection of our liberal religious heritage. The report then defended the postmodern demolition of the Enlightenment in a way that makes it sound like a creative opportunity. The report quotes Daniel Adams, a Presbyterian theologian teaching at Hanil Theological Seminary in Korea, when asked of the decline in the Western worldview, answered, "Could it not be nudging us in the direction of a more interconnected sense of life? Could it not bring us to the interdependent web of all existence of which we are a part?[137] In his defense of postmodernism Adams goes on to list its consequences to include.

> The creation of a new intellectual marketplace. Access to knowledge is no longer controlled by an academic or cultural elite. This means a far more diverse chorus of ideas and interpretations, all of which have equal claims to validity.[138]

Ironically, as we shall see in Chapter 8, "The Demolition of the Fourth Principle," in one of the programs at the 2020 General Assembly this same notion of all ideas having equal claim to validity is attributed to a deceptive use of free speech by conservatives and the alt-right. In this report from the 2005 Commission on Appraisal, however, the decline of the Western world view is portrayed as a creative opportunity. There might be a "new intellectual marketplace" where all ideas enjoy equal claims to validity because they could be free from the control of academia and cultural elites. This may sound like following through on our historic commitment to intellectual diversity, and that is the way this report meant to portray it. But it is not. Not at all. Within our liberal framework, all ideas do not have equal claim to validity. Ideas are equal only in the sense that they are all subject to the crucible of rational critique and debate; precisely because we believe that such a process leads to better ideas. This is the bedrock of our belief in progress. We believe democracy and free speech to be the most reliable path toward the betterment of humankind precisely because they institutionalize the virtues of rigorous criticism that the 2005 report depicts as controlling. As Ms. Pluckrose writes.

> Those modern ideas: reason, evidence, science, the marketplace of ideas, freedom of speech, the individual and liberal values applied consistently are the best of 500 years of intellectual and moral progress. They can be referred to as "the modernity project," "the Enlightenment project" or simply as "liberal secular democracy." We didn't get here quickly, and we didn't get here in a perfectly linear advancement of progress. But we got here.[139]

The 2005 Commission on Appraisal report, however, casts doubt on this core wisdom of our liberal faith.

> Postmodernism is a reaction against or a corrective to modernism. Modernism in theology can be very broadly characterized as a worldview based on an optimistic faith in progress and the rational pursuit of knowledge.
>
> Postmodern thinking, by contrast, asserts that it is hard to predict whether science will eventually save the world or destroy it.[140]

One might pause and wonder at the irony of this emerging skepticism about science, given that one of our Six Sources affirms and promotes "Humanist teachings which counsel us to heed the guidance of reason and the results of science, and warn us against the idolatries of mind and spirit." Be that as it may, by 2017, according to UU leadership, all ideas are not equal anyway. Because society is viewed as formed of systems of power and hierarchies, some ideas are clearly dominant, and for that reason oppressive, while all other ideas are for that reason marginalized and oppressed.

New UU Orthodoxy Is Beyond Criticism

Moreover, and importantly, this struggle to "decenter" or discard white ways of knowing and "center" and prioritize marginalized ways of knowing is quite beyond criticism. The resources we normally employ for critical purposes—rationality, science, evidence, and persuasion have all been relegated as tools of the dominant discourse of white Western ways of knowing. They are the tools of liberal oppression, and employing such resources for the sake of debate is itself viewed as supporting and advancing white supremacy. These methods, therefore, must be abandoned in favor of embracing the "lived experience." This is not to be mistaken for what we generally recognize as the knowledge most of us are said to acquire through our experience of life and occasionally sharing with others by way of imparting the wisdom of maturity or expertise. Rather, this is the lived experience of oppression, something only the marginalized have and only the marginalized understand and expressed in the stories of marginalized groups.

People not on the intersectionality scale, that is, the dominant group, are said not to experience oppression and therefore do not have what is meant here by lived experience. Neither, it is said, can they understand it. The best they can do, should they become "woke," is to realize and confess how it is that they participate in or are part of the dominant and oppressive liberal discourse. They should confess that they have been comfortable within that dominant discourse. They should become apologetic about being comfortable. They should try to persuade others that they too were born into the dominant discourse and are unaware of their own culpability in the oppression it breeds. Moreover, any distress or dissent at being told any of this is itself evidence that they are merely seeking to remain comfortable denizens within the oppressive system.

When it comes to how the world really works, something only the marginalized can really know, the voices of the marginalized must be regarded as authentic and authoritative in such a way as to preclude or prevent any disputes or questions about their understanding of any given situation or how to address it. To question is to invalidate their knowledge, their experience. Dissenting or critical voices are regarded as nothing more than disruptive, defensive or harmful. Harm, largely undefined, has become the moral high ground. The invocation of harm shuts down all dialogue. This is particularly distressing when in Chapter

8 we consider how the COIC report contains a recommendation to institutionalize monitoring the denomination in these terms.

In this connection, we should mention that to many critics this is the underlying premise of the book that is so central to the UUA's approach to anti-racism and anti-oppression, Robin DiAngelo's *White Fragility*, published by Beacon Press, the UUA's publishing arm.[141] Any response of white people to the charge of being white supremacists, other than apology, regret, and self-flagellation, is itself regarded as proof of the charge. When we combine this with the notion that the fight against oppression never ends, we get a glimpse of the kind of future this new orthodoxy holds for UUism.

None of this is meant to suggest that those who experience oppression do not have a special knowledge from that experience. Only a fool would deny it. In turn, none of this is to suggest that such experience is difficult to convey to those who do not have to live with it as part of their daily lives. Nor is any of this meant to suggest that those who do not live daily with oppression cannot by neglect unintentionally lend support to it. Rather, this is about how the experience of oppression is being weaponized against the very liberal values that supply legitimate avenues for redress. The greatest strength of Enlightenment modernity is arguably also its greatest weakness; that it allows its detractors to use the very freedoms it provides to oppose it. This illiberal liberatory theology does just that by using the very freedom our Enlightenment legacy provides to advance the case that the liberal order is itself the source of the oppression that the new illiberalism seeks to dismantle.

UU Leadership Seeks Authority and Power

We are now in a better position to understand the full meaning of the new liberatory theology that the UU leadership is working to establish as the new UU orthodoxy. This is a broad and far-reaching effort to move our denomination toward a more ecclesial rather than an associational religious institution. This implies the right to exercise coercive jurisdiction, to admonish UU members, ministerial or lay, who have not conformed to its view, and if needed to punish them. The trend here is simply unmistakable. There is an ever-increasing effort across the board to emphasize covenants that carry consequences for dissent, and to justify such consequences with re-interpretations of our principles, stressing community, responsibility, and "right relations" over conscience, congregational autonomy, and freedom. It is through this lens that we view the increasing stress of UU leadership on accountability through covenants, particularly ARAOMC (Anti-Racism, Anti-Oppression, Multi-Cultural), Right Relations covenants, and the proposed eighth principle.

> We, the member congregations of the Unitarian Universalist Association, covenant to affirm and promote journeying toward spiritual wholeness by working to build a diverse multicultural Beloved Community by our actions that accountably

dismantle racism and other oppressions in ourselves
and our institutions.

These covenants and this eighth principle seek to establish the
acceptable tone and content of our discourse and provide grounds for
the consequences of any offense or failure to comply. This is because
the Enlightenment discourse of reason, individual rights, science, and
evidence that undergirds our liberal faith has for UU leadership become
a threat to the moral imperative of anti-racism and anti-oppression
which has been declared as the core of our new liberatory theology.
Discourse must be monitored and transgressions punished. That is why
the COIC report and UU leadership talk so much about harm to the
marginalized without having to define what they mean by harm. Our
liberalism has become the harm.

We view this as tantamount to the rejection of our Seven
Principles.

Perhaps the most egregious episode that fully reveals what this
liberatory theology means for UUs is found in the way UU leadership
has treated one of its own. This is exceedingly clear from the
overwhelmingly irrational and irresponsible reaction leadership had
and continues to have to the publication of *The Gadfly Papers*. That
book questioned the very premises of the UU liberatory theology, using
Enlightenment methods of liberalism, logic, and reason, to do it. The
upshot was to publicly censure and finally dis-fellowship its author, Rev.
Dr. Todd Eklof. UU leadership has taken additional action to punish

those who defended that book and the right of the author to publish it. (This is thoroughly addressed in Chapter 8, "The Demolition of the Fourth Principle."

We at the Fifth Principle Project would not be at all surprised if this book, too, will be seen by leadership in the same terms, as little more than comfortable white men protecting and advancing the interests of white supremacy. Clearly, that is precisely the charge that one risks if one dissents from the new orthodoxy.

An Illiberal Theological Mandate

The COIC report portrays its recommendation for a theological mandate in terms of resurrecting and documenting "the words of Black people, Indigenous people, people of color, LGBTQ individuals, women and others who have been largely lost though their presence has been with us throughout history."[142] Likely there is not a UU alive who would ever argue with or oppose resurrecting valued voices of marginalized UU's and work to raise their visibility within our denomination. Neither would UU's deny that dramatically raising the profile of minority voices within our denomination is among our moral imperatives. The primary virtue of the new liberatory theology consists in its unwavering pursuit of this exceedingly worthy and laudable goal. But we believe that a "theological mandate" of any kind, much less one that abandons the liberal theology of our principles and sources and punishes principled dissent, would strike the average UU as oppressive and anti-Unitarian Universalist.

In the end, perhaps most Unitarian Universalists will choose to support the autocratic theological mandate UU leadership seeks to implement. But we at the Fifth Principle Project urge our readers to consider whether the goals of the UU leadership, as laudable and supportable as they are, can really be achieved by what are clearly illiberal means, by a theological mandate that does as much to silence some voices as it does to raise up others, and that is far more punitive than restorative. Liberatory theology is illiberal. It explicitly rejects the fruits of Enlightenment modernity that undergirds our UU faith, considering them at best naïve and simplistic and at worst, patriarchal, white supremacist, and imperialistic. This is not Unitarian Universalism. UUs have a choice to make, an historic choice. We urge all UU's to bring this conversation to their congregation for debate and if necessary, a vote. We at the Fifth Principle Project continue to have faith that our liberal theology is still the best guide we have toward a more progressive and inclusive future.

8.   The Demolition of the Fourth Principle

If we must give a platform and listen to every idea, there are no limits to the ideologies we must tolerate in the name of free speech.

Rev. Chris Rothbauer, "Building Communities to Counter White Nationalism/White Power," Program of the 2020 UUA General Assembly

---

The Real Meaning of Covenant and Accountability

We at the Fifth Principle Project believe that the UUA Board's embrace of liberatory theology means, in the end, the near-total rejection of the liberal Enlightenment modernity that undergirds our Seven Principles and Six Sources. We believe there is no more concrete and poignant expression of this drive toward "covenantal accountability" than the approach UU leadership has taken toward what is arguably the crown jewel of liberal democratic values—free speech.

Among the many insights Helen Pluckrose, a liberal humanist, author, and editor-in-chief of *Areo*, made in her essay *The Rise and Whys of Grievance Studies* are that in pre-Enlightenment times when blasphemy and heresy carried severe consequences, language was always inherently dangerous.[143] Such notions began to be overturned in the modern period. But as we argued in Chapter 7, according to the wokeism prevailing among the UU leadership, language has indeed become dangerous again. This was transparently exhibited in the effort of UU leadership to control what they regard as hate speech.

The basic approach is that to the extent free speech protects hate speech, free speech should be curtailed. As we shall see, this was the view in one of the programs presented at the 2020 General Assembly by Rev. Chris Rothbauer and Dr. Sharon Welsch. There is a perfectly legitimate public debate in our country about the extent to which free speech should protect hate speech. Curtailing free speech to prevent hate speech is not, however, a view held by most liberals. This is because it is often difficult to define hate speech. There is no legal definition of hate speech under U.S. law, just as there is no legal definition for evil ideas, rudeness, unpatriotic speech, or any other kind of speech that some may feel the need to curb. As we shall see, defining hate speech is a complicated problem when the intention is to prevent it.

This chapter concerns the way in which this issue has unfolded within UU leadership. While UU leadership tends to talk more in terms of harmful speech, they also tend to blur the difference between harmful and hate speech. The 2020 report from the Commission on Institutional Change talks about harmful speech. Rev. Rothbauer's program, discussed below, talks about hate speech. Neither harmful nor hate speech is ever actually defined, which may help explain why the boundaries are blurred. If free speech is to be in some way curbed to prevent hate speech, then it matters a great deal what hate speech is. If there is little or no real distinction made by UU leadership between hate speech and harmful speech, then the boundaries of the kinds of speech that UU leadership might seek to ban could be considerably expanded. This is critical for UUs to understand. There is nothing more illustrative of what this means for UUs than the response by leadership, particularly the Unitarian Universalist Ministers' Association (UUMA), to the publication of Rev. Dr. Eklof's book, *The Gadfly Papers*.

We must draw attention to the fact that the consequences for Rev. Dr. Eklof were that he was first publicly censured and ultimately dis-fellowshipped from the UU ministry for the publication of his book. The reason for the censure was stated in the first line of the UUMA's censure letter. "We are writing this letter of censure regarding the content and the manner of distribution (at the 2019 General Assembly) of your book, *The Gadfly Papers*." The letter then claims that the content of the book "has caused great psychological, spiritual, and emotional damage for many individuals and communities within our faith."[144] Nothing specific that Rev. Eklof wrote in his book was cited in the UUMA censure letter.

Despite the alleged harm caused by the book, Dr. Eklof's disfellowship was not due to anything he wrote. Rather, the Ministerial Fellowship Committee (MFC) claimed he was out of covenant by failing to cooperate in its investigation and thus took action to remove him from the rolls of the MFC. There is ample evidence, however, that Rev. Dr. Eklof did indeed engage with the MFC. In his forthcoming book *The Gadfly Affair*, Rev. Dr. Eklof will provide both a detailed account as well as documentation of his interaction with the UU leadership and the MFC. We will let that book speak for itself. What is germane to this discussion on freedom of speech was the rush to judgment by officially affiliated UU organizations that issued open condemnatory letters shortly after the distribution of *The Gadfly Papers* at the 2019 Spokane General Assembly. These open letters accused Rev. Dr. Eklof of harmful speech with others going so far as to indicate that *The Gadfly Papers* was violent speech and still others indicating it was hate speech. Hate speech as Rev. Rothbauer argued in his program must be prevented for the sake of beloved community.

Consider, for one prominent example, the June 2019 letter from 500 ministers.

> Instead of accepting the frame of Rev. Eklof's arguments and debunking them, we instead affirm the following: White Supremacy Culture (WSC) is alive and well within Unitarian Universalism. . . This treatise, itself, is a manifestation of WSC, and is causing harm to our siblings of color, as well as to the integrity of our ministry.
>
> Ideas and language can indeed be **forms of violence** and can cause real harm . . . The predictable **"freedom of speech" arguments are commonly weaponized** to perpetuate oppression and inflict further harm.[145] (bold added)

After condemning Rev. Dr. Eklof's entire book as nothing more than an example of white supremacy culture, this letter went on to make two assertions critical to the argument of condemnation, assertions the authors of the letter hoped would go unchallenged. One, they were quick to extend the idea of harmful speech to violent speech. Others would extend harmful speech directly to hate speech. This need to escalate their accusations to the extreme is essential to the second assertion, that any debate over "freedom of speech" should be rejected when unwanted speech is involved. The letter posited that since harmful/violent/hate speech is involved, then freedom of speech cannot be used to defend such speech. In this context, freedom of speech becomes a weapon to "perpetuate oppression and inflict further harm." These assertions lack any factual basis and are self-serving on the part of UU leadership.

As noted earlier, at no time do Dr. Eklof's critics ever define harmful, violent, or hate speech. Others, however, have not been so reluctant to define hate speech. The Cambridge dictionary defines hate speech as "public speech that expresses hate or encourages violence towards a person or group based on something such as race, religion, sex, or sexual orientation." In an article for Britannia, William M. Curtis, Assistant Professor of Political Science, University of Portland, defines hate speech as involving "epithets and slurs, statements that promote malicious stereotypes, and speech intended to incite hatred or violence against a group." Moreover, while the Supreme Court has ruled in *Matal v. Tam* that there is no hate speech exception to free speech, inciting violence with hate speech is illegal and actionable. Therefore, we think using the term violence in connection with Dr. Eklof's book at the very least obscures what is meant by harmful speech. More importantly, associating Rev. Dr. Eklof's book with violence suggests that his book is not just harmful speech, but hate speech.

Another letter from the Allies for Racial Equity (ARE) pushed the boundaries of harmful speech by attempting to directly align Rev. Dr. Eklof's words with hate speech that is frequently associated with the alt-right.

> This book is not only a failed attempt at logical discourse rife with white fragility, [it is] a stark reminder that **ideas aligned with alt-right ideology do exist within Unitarian Universalism**. It is a clear premeditated and callous attempt to further strife within our beloved faith. It has caused and is causing pain to all too many within our UU community. It is a manifestation of white supremacy culture fighting back against the beautiful, transformative work that so many are doing to confront and dismantle systems of oppression.[146] (bold added)

The assertion that Rev. Dr. Eklof's book is aligned with alt-right ideology explicitly declares that the book crosses the line from harmful to hate speech. This is critically important because as we shall see, this places *The Gadfly Papers* in a class of speech that, according to Rev. Rothbauer, needs to be prevented.

Let us pause and consider the gravity of what UU leadership is saying. First, without any specifics, UU leadership alleges that *The Gadfly Papers* is harmful speech. Such a charge requires a coherent argument, and a coherent argument requires specificity. The absence of specificity renders the charge of harm hollow. Second, escalating the accusation by associating the book with violent speech, albeit emotional stress, is a more serious allegation. Again, absent any specific citation to support such a grave charge substitutes hyperbole for thoughtful engagement. To suggest the book is hate speech without a coherent case based on specifics amounts to a deliberate smear and is irresponsible on the part of our UU leadership.

General Assembly 2020 and Free Speech

Curtailing hate speech was among the primary concerns of one of the programs of General Assembly 2020, "Building Communities to Counter White Nationalism/White Power," presented by Rev. Chris Rothbauer and Dr. Sharon Welsch. This program was almost completely focused on finding ways to limit the presence of conservative and alleged alt-right speech within the UU faith community. More disturbingly for liberals was that the program made the argument that UUs at least (and the country by implication) are morally obligated to deny a platform to ideas that are regarded as hate speech because they are harmful to the marginalized. This denial, the program argued, should be pursued for the sake of the beloved community. In an example of how leadership is trying to re-interpret our principles in terms of the beloved community, Rev. Rothbauer even proclaims that this moral obligation to curtail free speech to exclude hate speech is already in our principles. In one of his slides he declared, "This is already enshrined in Unitarian Universalism's Fifth Principle: A free and responsible search for truth and meaning."

While Rothbauer identified the wrong principle, which should have been the Fourth and not the Fifth principle, the point was clear. This was an attempt at a complete re-interpretation of the Fourth Principle to mean refusing a platform to ideas UU leadership finds objectionable, harmful, or views as hate speech. Rather, the generally accepted interpretation of our Fourth Principle is that UUs are morally obligated to vigorously oppose and counter such ideas with more and better speech. At least, that would be the liberal interpretation. The answer of liberals to alt-right hate speech is more free speech based on our principles. "When they go low," as Michelle Obama declared, "we go high."

Sources of Hate Speech

In addition to advocating the curtailing of free speech to prevent hate speech, the program also dwelt a good deal on the sources of hate speech and how such speech manages to find its way to the mainstream and into communities like that of Unitarian Universalism. The program identified the source of hate speech to be white nationalism. Dr. Sharon Welsch gave a summation of who white nationalists are and what they believe, all anathema to UU beliefs. Summarized in one of the slides used by Rev. Rothbauer, these ideas are pretty much the same kind of ideas, racist and sexist, that Rev. Dr. Eklof was accused of representing in all the letters of condemnation issued by UU leadership in response.

According to Rev. Rothbauer, the prime conduit of hate speech into the mainstream is through the deceptive use of free speech by conservatives. By deceptive we mean that for Rothbauer, conservatives have developed a technique to use free speech as a vehicle to support hate speech. It is based on a well-known thesis that conservatives blunt or dismiss any criticism of their ideas by claiming to be victims of cancel culture, otherwise known as political correctness. This is the tactic Rev. Rothbauer said wealthy conservatives like the Koch brothers have employed to get their unpopular and often discredited ideas publicly entertained, particularly on college campuses. It has also been the model emulated by white nationalists. Rothbauer believes this technique has introduced an era of what he called "absolute free speech" in which all ideas have "equal worth and dignity," and where all ideologies, including the hate speech of the white nationalist alt-right, are afforded equal time in "the marketplace of ideas." Hence the quote from one of Rev. Rothbauers' slides at the beginning of this chapter.

Rothbauer later equivocated in the program to deny that all ideas have "equal worth and dignity." The reality, however, is that ideas never had equal worth and dignity in the marketplace of free speech. Free speech has always been about debating ideas, discerning bad from good from better ideas. Even if alt-righters use a deceptive appeal to free speech to get themselves heard, the deception is at least an implicit acknowledgment of this truth.

Nonetheless, Rothbauer correctly said that it is under cover of this weaponized form of free speech that the alt-right advances its racist and sexist agenda. The question is, what does this have to do with the UU faith community? The answer is that since UU leadership has repeatedly accused Rev. Dr. Eklof of advancing alt-right ideology, the clear implication is that he did so by way of a deceptive appeal to free speech. This charge was echoed in the letter from 500 white Unitarian Universalist ministers. "The predictable 'freedom of speech' argument is commonly weaponized to perpetuate oppression and inflict further harm."[147]

Therefore, not only did UU leadership declare *The Gadfly Papers* to be advancing an alt-right ideology, but they charged Rev. Dr. Eklof with using the same deceptive method of the alt-right to get his criticisms of UU leadership heard. Rev. Rothbauer's program suggested that, for the sake of the beloved community, neither should have happened and should never happen again.

UU Liberalism as the Source of Oppressive Hate Speech

It is important to reiterate that Rev. Dr. Eklof's book has been declared by UU leadership to be aligned with alt-right ideology, and they have accused Rev. Dr. Eklof of deception to perpetuate his alleged alt-right ideology. UUs should wonder why a UU minister who as a matter of public record has supported and advanced our liberal religious tradition, stands accused by his own leadership of representing the same kind of ideas as the alt-right. UUs should ask their leadership to explain this charge and to show how Rev. Dr. Eklof is guilty of the same kind of deceptive delivery method employed by the alt-right. Moreover, if UU leadership never defines hate speech, how can they accuse Rev. Dr. Eklof of using an appeal to free speech to protect hate speech? Could it be because in the new UU liberatory theology the liberal tradition, known as UUism, the tradition that Rev Dr. Eklof defended in the section of his book entitled *"The Religion of Humanity"*[148] has become, or is coming to be regarded as hate speech?

We at the Fifth Principle Project believe the answer to the above question is yes. We believe this helps explain why UU leadership has failed to be specific about what in *The Gadfly Papers* merits the charges they have persistently leveled at Rev. Dr. Eklof. We believe that criticizing UU leadership from within our liberal religious tradition is seen now as a form of hate speech that is harmful to the marginalized of our faith community and therefore must be punished.

We are, moreover, concerned that in their rush to impose the kind of accountability we have been describing in this chapter, this has become a matter of policy. Certainly, Rev. Dr. Eklof has not been the only minister to have been disciplined for speaking their mind about the direction in which the UU leadership seeks to take us. Rev. Rick Davis, for example, was removed from his position of UU Good Officer for defending Dr. Eklof and criticizing the actions of the UUMA. See chapter 10 in this book for more information. Rev. Mel Pine was punished for his criticism of the direction the UUA is taking.[149] Other ministers have been removed from the UUMA's Facebook page for expressing views critical of the UUMA, the latest as of this writing is Rev. Kate Rhode (See Chapter 13, "Accusation and Polarization II"). In this connection, we draw your attention to the letter, "We Quit" (See Appendix D) written to the UUMA by ministers who have resigned in protest of the UUMA's effort to impose accountability on ministers. They cite, among other reasons:

> Some of the new offenses outlined in the Code are outrageous, if not patently absurd . . . Language

throughout the new Code conveys the implicit presumption of guilt . . . [and] Perhaps most shocking is the complete elimination of due process in the enforcement of our Code.

Though these new rules were adopted by the UUMA in 2020, their breathtaking overreach was applied before their formal adoption. Rev. Richard Trudeau received a censure letter in 2018 from the UUMA for unspecified complaints that had been made about his posts on the UUMA Facebook page. See Chapter 11 for more information. Rev. Trudeau wrote three letters of inquiry about the accusations and the rationale behind the letter of censure, but never received a reply. Another minister was accused of unspecified charges by a fellow minister. (See Chapter 12, "Accusation and Polarization I") We should underscore that all of these incidents, and others, involve principled disagreement with and legitimate criticism of the direction of UU leadership.

The Expansion of Accountability

This trend of demanding more accountability from UU's who are doing nothing more than speaking their minds involves lay people as well. We know of one 50-year Unitarian Universalist who was ejected from her congregation, and other long-time lay Unitarian Universalists who have been on the receiving end of disciplinary actions from their congregations. The dramatic expansion of accountability is embedded in some of the recommendations from the Commission on Institutional Change. Consider the following recommendations.

Recommendation

Accountability should be embedded in the structure of the Boards of the Association and other key organizations, including all affiliated and professional organizations.

For equity, inclusiveness, and diversity to flourish in our Association, a united commitment must be reflected in the identity documents of the Association and all affiliate organizations. The differing practices and levels of commitment from structural entity to structural entity within our Association is one of the ways Black people, Indigenous people, people of color, and members of other historically marginalized groups are injured over and over again . . .

This recommendation tells us that UU leadership intends to impose the kind of accountability we have seen in this chapter on the entire institutional structure of our denomination, "from structural entity to structural entity" (meaning congregations and fellowships) eliminating "differing practices and levels of commitment." This one recommendation alone spells the end of congregational autonomy. The peculiar practices of any given congregation, their kinds of worship, internal programming, and activism will be evaluated in terms of how well they conform to whatever comes from the UUA, as will their level of commitment to this new UU orthodoxy.

It spells the end of individual conscience as well, because no UU will be able to enjoy a leadership position within their congregation, nor form an affiliated organization devoted to a specific purpose without explicit conformity to this new UU orthodoxy. It is already this way in some congregations.

Recommendation

Ongoing monitoring is needed to ensure that work to counter bias and oppression is not interrupted again.

This recommendation concerns the creation and implementation of some kind of mechanism for ongoing monitoring. In an action item following this recommendation, it is urged that this monitoring should be included in the bylaws of the denomination and every congregation. It is a bit difficult to tell just how this would work, but the important point here is that if this is implemented, your congregation will be watched, and, in turn, your congregation will watch you. Everyone will be watched for the level of their commitment and conformity to the new UU orthodoxy. In another subsequent action item, it tells us reports should be made. Given what we have already seen, there can be little doubt that those reports will carry consequences. It is difficult to imagine anything more objectionable to the liberal Unitarian Universalism that we have known. But you must remember that the liberal version of our faith is now accused of being the source of our sins against the marginalized and needs to be abandoned.

This intention to implement monitoring for conformance to the New Orthodoxy is underscored in the last recommendation, an independent board-level body constituted by members of marginalized groups who will monitor accountability across the country.

Recommendation

> The UUA should establish an ongoing independent body to identify systemic changes and monitor accountability on work toward equity, inclusion, and diversity. This body should be based on representatives of groups of oppressed people and should have direct representation on the Association Board.

If this recommendation is any measure of how this will work, we will be asked to simply trust the testimony of each member of this board-level group as to what on any given occasion they might find hurtful, traumatizing, or marginalizing. Why? As the letter from 500 white ministers said, because white supremacy patriarchy is the default, and the UUA Board trusts that the marginalized alone know what it is to be victims of it. With all due respect for trusting the experience of others, ask yourself, is it trust that UU leadership is requiring of us, or obedience? We believe it is far more likely obedience than trust, and obedience has never been listed among the virtues of Unitarian Universalism.

We believe that in the New Orthodoxy, because the default is white supremacist patriarchy, dissenting views are to be condemned and punished precisely because they are dissenting. This to us means obedience under cover of the beloved community. It helps explain why none of the critics of *The Gadfly Papers* ever specified precisely what in the book is so traumatizing, nor are they required to do so by UU leadership. As we argued in Chapter 7, "The New Orthodoxy," just asking for an explanation is itself regarded as an example of white supremacy inflicting further injury. Even inquiring about how we are supposed to know that any accusations that might be made are accurate is felt to be inflicting further injury because asking the question is said to force the marginalized to relive the painful experience.

We at the Fifth Principle Project do not doubt that the marginalized do suffer from oppression. We are concerned, however, that the approach of UU leadership puts us all into one hell of a bind. It bifurcates us irreconcilably into at least two unbridgeable tribes, the oppressed and the oppressors. The oppressors are told they should assume a permanent posture of apology and perpetual shame which, in a nutshell, suggests pretty much what it will be like for many of us within this new UU orthodoxy.

Epilogue

In June 2018, Rev. Meg Riley, one of the two new co-moderators, hosted a video program that is part of a series called *The VUU,* a Unitarian Universalist talk platform. About 11 minutes into VUU #185, "Intentionally Radical and Spiritual Spaces", (We do not know if this is still available online.), Rev. Riley and a colleague have an exchange over a question posed by Rev. Riley as to what the participants meant by the terms "radical" vs. "liberal." What follows is a transcript of that exchange.

Meg Riley to Rev. Ashley Haram:

> Take a second, Ashley, 'cause people use these words all the time. I'm curious what you mean when you say liberal and radical . . . not to, you know, write a dissertation, but just a sentence, about each.

Ashley:

> Yeah, I mean I think for me when I use the term radical I think I mean understanding that we live in a world that is dominated by systems of oppression and that it requires a frame of collective liberation for all of us to move to a different kind of world, dismantling systems of oppression and creating new ones that are

different than what we've been living in for the past several thousand years of history.

Liberalism for me is a lot about like buying into capitalism and sort of understanding that there are problems in the world, but often having a more reformist approach rather than like let's create something entirely new kind of approach. People who are political scientists will do a much better job explaining this to me but that's it.

Meg Riley:

Well then, thanks, I appreciate that. I think about it in the garden . . . radical comes from roots and I think about these weeds that I have . . . and unless I dig them up from the roots which often means sadly pulling up plants I love, and either painstakingly sorting through or ditching the whole thing, and it takes a lot of time to do that painstaking sorting out, and I'll say, having done it about four times within one week that I have, it doesn't just happen once, but anyway that's how I've been thinking 'bout radical lately.

So I was curious, whereas I have this other policy I call sanctions, which is where I just deprive things of light and I know it won't kill them, the roots are still there, but at least they're not getting more light. That's a gardener's perspective. I think that what you're talking about is systemic disruption, and anyway, just giving you a chance to breathe air.

Before her acclamation to the position of co-moderator, the Fifth Principle Project emailed Rev. Riley asking about these comments. (Our apologies if "her" is the wrong pronoun.) We also posted to Facebook and directed both co-moderators to the page, so that they could provide comments. We never got a reply

What garden is being discussed in this casual metaphor? Could it be the Unitarian Universalist community? Yes, since this is a UU talk program, and since two UU ministers are talking about liberals vs. radicals, it is safe to say it very well could be. Who are the weeds that need to be removed from this garden? Are they the liberals of our faith community? Yes, it seems safe to say that in this garden metaphor liberals are the weeds needing removal. It seems that the liberals are to be painstakingly sorted through, "dug up by the roots." Or, if it takes too much time and trouble, then they are to simply be deprived of light, whatever that may mean, to keep them from growing. In either case, the metaphor of the garden seems to mean that liberals need to be somehow eliminated from Unitarian Universalism. We at the Fifth Principle Project regard this metaphor as an apt summation of the current intent of UU leadership. It is a clear message that if you oppose their methods, then you oppose their goals. We at the Fifth Principle Project viscerally but respectfully disagree.

Unitarian Universalists are being faced with monumentally important choices about the kind of faith community we want to be. We are asking you all to think about this and discuss it with your fellow congregants. We are urging you to become more involved with what is happening to our denomination. Become informed delegates to the General Assembly and take this debate to leadership. We at the Fifth Principle Project cleave to a faith in our liberal Enlightenment heritage and to our principles birthed in that heritage as still the best path forward to a more inclusive faith community.

Governance

9.   21st Century Fifth Principle

Despite having a principle affirming our belief in the use of democracy within our congregations and society at large, Unitarian Universalism is really in the backwaters of democracy at the national level. Although both local congregations and our national denomination rely on representative democracy with the election of individuals, whether trustees or delegates, to represent a larger body of UUs, at the national level there are structural and cultural problems that have resulted in our denominational governance becoming a representative democracy in name only. For most UUs, our focus is on our congregations, where we have congregational meetings in which we debate and vote on key issues and elect leaders. Our congregational leaders mingle, listen, and acknowledge the concerns of their fellow congregants. We would like to think the same is going on at the national level, but it is not.

In Chapter 2, "Fifth Principle Task Force" we examined the UUA's governance structure, summarized here for convenience. At the Association level, there are two governing bodies, the UUA Board of Trustees and the General Assembly. The UUA Board of Trustees governs the Association between General Assemblies. At General Assembly, governance of the Association shifts to congregational delegates, who cast votes regarding the election of the denomination's president and other initiatives that have been placed on the agenda by the Board of Trustees. This governance model should, in theory, provide an efficient way to manage the affairs of the Association. The Board of Trustees manages the day-to-day affairs and General Assembly gives congregations a voice in governance where board recommendations can either be accepted or rejected.

Unfortunately, the reality is quite different from the theory. General Assembly, as a representative body of congregations, has long been recognized as "broken." It has been nearly a decade since the shortcomings of General Assembly were identified by the Fifth Principle Task Force. The problems include the poor participation of congregations, the dearth of knowledgeable delegates, and the discriminatory nature of the gathering due to cost and time. We at the Fifth Principle Project also believe that our other national governing body, the UUA Board of Trustees, is unresponsive and unaccountable.

Consider this one clause buried in the Association bylaws in Article IX, Nominations and Elections, in section 9.10 subsection (a), which reads ". . . if only one person has been validly nominated for each elected position at large the persons so nominated shall be declared elected and no ballots shall be required." The Nominating Committee is under no obligation to present more than one candidate for an elected position, which means that the Nominating Committee is essentially selecting the members of the UUA Board of Trustees.

Recovering our democracy will not be easy, and it will not happen overnight.

The Purpose of the Unitarian Universalist Association

Before discussing how we can better govern the Association, let us first consider the purpose of the Association. To be clear, the purpose of the Unitarian Universalist Association is not a mystery. It has been consistently articulated since the merger. The first line in the current bylaws regarding the purpose of the Association states that the UUA "shall devote its resources and exercise its corporate powers for religious, educational and humanitarian purposes."[150] That statement from our current bylaws is nearly identical to the original 1961 Constitution phrasing, ". . . for religious, educational and charitable purposes." As we discussed in the Article II Study Commission chapter, in 1985 the wording was extended to read, "The primary purpose of the Association is to serve the needs of its member congregations, organize new congregations, extend and strengthen Unitarian Universalist institutions and implement its principles." What exactly are the actions being taken by our UU leadership to fulfill this mandate?

There has been a consistent message from the Association's President, Rev. Susan Frederick-Gray, expressed in both her speeches and written communications, that the mission of the UUA staff is to equip congregations, train and credential leaders, and advance UU values in the wider world. That general mission statement can take on many forms in the actual implementation. For example, in the

169

President's budget submission memo in April 2020 the implementation of the mission statement is interpreted to mean "dismantling white supremacy and patriarchy and advancing equity and liberation within and beyond our faith community."

The $17,000,000 in the President's submitted budget for the fiscal year 2021-2022 is a substantial amount. In pre-COVID years budgets have been higher. Through the Annual Program Fund (APF), our congregation payments sent to Boston provide a large share of the money spent on our behalf, making our congregations, on a financial basis alone, the primary shareholder in the UUA. We at the Fifth Principle, however, do not feel that we are getting "value for money." More importantly, we do not believe the bylaws-mandated purpose of the Association to serve the needs of its member congregations and advance UUism is fulfilled by our UU leadership diverting our resources into a self-declared internal crisis regarding UUism's complicity with white supremacy.

So, what can we do? We at the Fifth Principle Project believe that a return to governance based on a functioning democracy will enable the Association to resume focus on its primary purpose. The re-introduction of democracy will require changes in at least two areas: leadership culture and bylaws changes.

Leadership Culture

For more than a decade there has been an ever-growing entrenchment in UU leadership culture that has advocated for more centralized power in Boston. With bylaws changes to the nomination and election processes, the UUA Board now literally has the ability to self-select its members and has achieved the concern expressed at the 2011 Charlotte General Assembly: "We want more delegate choice, not the selection by a nominating committee . . . We can do better than an inbred power structure."

The UUA Board of Trustees has become an entity unto itself, with no real accountability to UUs across the country. It will take a great deal of introspective thinking by our leadership to see how far they have fallen from UU liberal values and the upholding of the primary purpose of the Association. Unitarian Universalism does not belong to the UUA Board, the president, the moderator, any advocacy group, or person. It belongs to all UUs, who have a right, enshrined in our principles, to participate in the governance of the denomination.

It is unrealistic to think that our UU leadership will experience a collective epiphany and spontaneously begin the needed introspective conversation. Power once achieved is not lightly relinquished. Conversations will need to start in our own congregations about the role or relevance of the UUA and how we, the governed, wish to entrust our authority in our national leadership. Those congregational conversations will need to be raised upward to our national UU leadership. If we don't have consensus on the nature of our governance structure and that the power to govern is derived from our congregations and granted upward to our UU leadership, none of the next steps regarding real institutional change through bylaws updates will be possible.

How to Amend our Bylaws

Updates to the Association's bylaws will take the most effort but will return the greatest benefit. Our bylaws contain not only our principles in Article II but the nuts and bolts of the governance of the denomination in other articles and rules. At the time of the merger, the denomination was governed by two documents, a Constitution and a set of bylaws. In 1972 these two documents were merged into a single document, henceforth to be referenced only as bylaws. The original Constitution's articles merged into the new bylaws document preserved their provenance by having a "C" appended. That is why the section in Article II that contains our principles is labeled Section C-2.1, known as a "C Bylaw."

Amending our bylaws, by design, is a lengthy process that requires in the end a vote at a General Assembly. The process for amending "C Bylaws" has its own process. An amendment may be submitted by the Board of Trustees, a General Assembly Planning Committee, a Commission on Appraisal, fifteen certified member congregations, or a district or region at a duly called meeting. The last option, to submit an amendment by a district or region, requires that a district or region have a formal governance structure, or that the amendment be presented at a meeting convened by fifteen congregations "in good standing with the UUA." Amendments must be submitted to the UUA Board of Trustees.[151] Once submitted to the Board of Trustees, the proposed change to the bylaws is added to the tentative agenda for the General Assembly.[152] The process then follows the rules established for running the General Assembly.

General Assembly Delegates

From the very founding of the Universalist and Unitarian denominations, General Assemblies or conventions have been delegate-based. The formula for delegate allocation established in the 1961 bylaws has remained largely intact. Although there have been some adjustments made in the allocation ranges, the basic formula has been unchanged, awarding the number of delegates by dividing the number of members in a congregation by 50. There are special allocation structures for the Church of the Larger Fellowship[153] as well as a concept that empowers the Association to confer delegate status on ministers, religious educators, and those with emeritus/emerita status who meet specific criteria. Those with voting rights at General Assembly include delegates appointed by a congregation and qualified religious professionals.[154]

Eliminate External Appointment of Delegates

The first change that needs to be made to reclaim our democracy is the elimination of delegate preference given to clergy and educators by the Association's bylaws. Those serving our congregations have special privileges and freedoms within our congregations. That status should remain at the local congregational level, and there is no reason to extend this special status to the national level. All UUs should be equal when it comes to voting at General Assembly. Congregations may choose, at their discretion, to extend delegate status to the minister or educator from their pool of allocated General Assembly delegates. Let's consider three problems with the Association's bylaws conferring delegate status to ministers and educators.

The first problem is that allowing an external entity to grant delegate status to a person in a congregation is inconsistent with the democratic right of a congregation to elect or appoint its own delegates. That is, based on congregational polity, congregations have the right to govern the affairs of their congregation without the intervention of the Association. Congregations can call their own ministers, so why can't congregations name all of their own General Assembly delegates? Nonetheless, Article IV General Assembly, Section 4.8 allows the Association to confer delegate status on a congregation's ministers and educators without the consent of the congregation.

Second, there is a potential for creating a super delegate "voting bloc" formed around a shared interest. The event at the 2019 General Assembly when 300 to 500 ministers rapidly coordinated to submit a letter of condemnation of Rev. Dr. Todd Eklof regarding his book *The Gadfly Papers* illustrates the real potential for professionals to act on a shared interest, regardless of the support from the laity for their actions. A source of this shared interest is inherent in the bylaws requirement that delegate status for the clergy and educators be dependent on holding specific professional association credentials. A minister must be in fellowship with the Association granted through the Ministerial Fellowship Committee (MFC) and an educator must be an active member in the Liberal Religious Educator Association (LREDA).[155] Each of these organizations may have its own objectives or agendas regarding the business before the General Assembly.

Finally, there is a possibility that professional associations may exert either real or perceived influence over the employment or professional career path of an individual regarding a General Assembly vote. Even the appearance of influence creates an unhealthy situation both for the individual and for the integrity of the General Assembly voting process.

Direct Electors vs. Delegate Electors

The second change is to reconsider why decisions that should be made by all UUs are made only by congregational delegates. A model for this change is the 17th Amendment to the U.S. Constitution, which empowers citizens to directly elect their U.S. Senators, overturning the mechanism first written in the U.S. Constitution that gave that power to state legislatures. Defining which issues should be decided by all UUs will take a fair amount of debate, but decisions made about Article II, which contains our principles, sources, the purpose of the Association, and freedom of belief statement, impact all UUs and thus would be appropriate for an all-UU vote. With current technology, we have it within our power to engage all UUs, but do we have the will to do so?

Other issues to be considered for a popular vote by all UUs include the election of our denomination's president and moderator. We have seen in our recent U.S. presidential contests the election of individuals (George Bush and Donald Trump) who won the Electoral College but failed to win the popular vote. We think most UUs feel, as we do, that a democratic popular vote is more representative of the "will of the people" than an artificially created Electoral College. There may be insufficient political consensus in the U.S. to overturn the Electoral College, but UUs have within us the power to have a popular vote on important issues.

Fortunately, Article IX in our bylaws already contains provisions for mail and electronic balloting that may be the mechanism for extending voting rights to all UUs. To be clear, all UUs means all UUs. Careful wording is required to determine voting eligibility, such as membership in a congregation, fellowship, or Church of the Larger Fellowship. The intent, however, is clear: Engage all UUs in issues that impact all UUs. If you recall, in 2009 only 0.7% of UUs decided the fate of proposed changes to Article II. Consideration will be required on the percentage of affirmative votes required to pass a particular "all UU" vote, whether plurality, majority, two-thirds, etc. The leap forward is to empower UUs in the decisions that have a material impact on the nature of the Association and the principles of UUism.

Other issues can continue to be voted upon in a reformed representative democracy structure at General Assembly. A reformed General Assembly is dependent on implementing key Fifth Principle Task Force recommendations, without delay, regarding the early selection of General Assembly delegates and the scheduling of work sessions so General Assembly delegates can be educated on the issues to be decided at the collective gathering of congregational delegates.

The success of this reintroduction of democracy in the governance of the denomination rests on the rejection of the *laissez-faire* attitude within our congregations over the selection of General Assembly delegates and the charging of those delegates to vote per the instructions from the congregation. This charging of delegates by a congregation also addresses a current General Assembly shortcoming regarding the knowledge of delegates on the business to be decided at the Assembly. To charge a delegate, the congregation's members will also need to become aware of the Assembly's business and the implications of a yea or nay vote. General Assembly must be viewed not as an assembly of individuals, but as an assembly of congregational delegates.

Likewise, our UU leadership must end its *laissez-faire* attitude regarding congregational delegate attendance at General Assembly. No longer can our leadership be content to have decisions made for the whole denomination simply by the delegates who "showed up." We know from the Fifth Principle Task Force Report that 40% of the

Association's member congregations do not fully participate in General Assembly. To correct this problem a quorum should be established at General Assembly based on the total allocation of General Assembly delegates. This requirement will add a burden to our leadership to encourage, cajole, or incentivize congregations to send delegates to General Assembly. For General Assembly to live up to its ideal as a representative body of congregational delegates, more work is needed by everyone.

Competitive Elections

A small change to Article IX Nominations and Elections in section 9.10 subsection (a), referenced earlier, could have a significant impact on the election of UU leadership. The article includes a section that states that if there is no opposing candidate for an at-large elective office then "no voting shall be required." The change offered by the Fifth Principle Project is that all at-large elective offices must be elected and face, at a minimum, a vote known as "no confidence." With competitive elections, even against a stand-in "no-confidence candidate," candidates would then have an incentive to present their qualifications and platform to General Assembly delegates. Delegates would have an opportunity, currently denied, to support a candidate or register their dissatisfaction with a vote of no confidence. This change goes a long way toward striking down the preemptive power of the Nominating Committee to offer a slate of candidates without opposition.

Nomination by Petition

Our bylaws provide opportunities for grassroots initiatives to put candidates and bylaws changes before the General Assembly for a vote by petition. The signature requirement for a petition, for example, for a candidate for the UUA Board of Trustees is not burdensome, requiring only fifty signatures with no more than ten signatures from a single congregation. To guide candidates through the petition process there is a page on the UUA website that provides an overview of the process as well as access to downloadable forms required by the process.

Restructure Election of Board of Trustees

The UUA Board of Trustees has enormous explicit and discretionary powers and has become, in the opinion of the Fifth Principle Project, unresponsive to UUs in our congregations. A dramatic restructuring of that body is needed to restore accountability. The essence of this recommendation is a recognition that changes made in 2011 that eliminated locally elected trustees, the designation of trustees to at-large, and the use of a centralized nominating committee to select trustee candidates have resulted in the erosion of the democracy in the governance of the denomination.

Prior to the 2011 change to our bylaws, the UUA Board of Trustees was composed of the president, moderator, three to four at-large trustees elected at General Assembly, and local trustees who were nominated and elected by the districts. The changes to this process in 2011 successfully reduced the size of the UUA Board of Trustees. That success should not be undone. However, the concept of a board with only at-large trustees needs to be revisited. A good starting point is to reconsider the pre-2011 model when the board was composed of a mixture of at-large and local trustees. Absent our 19-district structure, our current 5-region organization structure could be the new basis for local democracy. A rough formula for UUA Board membership allocation could include three at-large trustees identified by a modified nominating committee and elected at General Assembly and two or three UUA trustees nominated and elected by the regions.

Recall that among the motivations for creating a nominating committee was to elect board members who reflect "the full diversity of the Association, especially in regard to historically marginalized communities." There is no easy answer to achieving goals of diversity and democracy but presenting such goals as mutually exclusive is a mistake. There is always a battle to be fought for equality. Add that there is now a battle to be fought for democracy.

Disciplining of Ministers

One final comment regarding restoring control to our local autonomous congregations and accountability to our UU leadership teams. Since 2017 we have seen actions taken by the Unitarian Universalist Ministers' Association (UUMA) and the UUA Ministerial Fellowship Committee (MFC) to censure and to dis-fellowship ministers for questioning the character of the denomination as portrayed by our UU leadership. Chapters 10, 11, 12, and 13 address encounters ministers have had with national administrative entities.

The chapters noted above raise the question: What consent must an administrative body such as the UUMA and MFC receive from a congregation before it takes action against a congregation's minister? Within our congregations, ministers are granted freedom of the pulpit. There is no caveat to that grant of pulpit freedom that an external agency can terminate a privilege given a minister by their congregation. As a denomination devoted to our faith in conscience and free expression, we should protect the right of our ministers to speak, even challenge, ideas that they deem important to their ministry.

Unfortunately, our national leadership bodies have not respected the freedoms that congregations have granted their ministers. Our leadership has not sought consent from congregations before initiating action against a congregational minister. This model of unilateral action runs counter to our tradition of congregational autonomy and congregational polity. That is, congregations are free to call and dismiss their ministers without seeking consent from any national administrative body. Why then do entities external to our congregations grant themselves the authority to operate independently over our congregations?

There is an argument for the denomination to have some disciplinary authority to ensure that our ministers conduct themselves with the highest level of professional behavior. Such external

181

disciplinary authority is needed if a congregation fails to recognize or respond to the behavior of a minister regarding sexual, financial, or other egregious behavior. Simply voicing dissent, writing a book, or asking questions on Facebook are not sufficiently egregious acts to invoke a rebuke from a national administrative entity.

10. Good Officer Account

By Rev. Richard Read Davis

Before joining fourteen other UU ministers in September 2020 when we resigned in protest from the Unitarian Universalist Ministers' Association (UUMA), I served as a Good Officer in the UUMA's Pacific Northwest Chapter, having been elected by my colleagues to that position on four separate occasions during my 27 years as a settled minister in Salem, Oregon. A Good Officer advocates for the prerogatives of UU ministers and offers pastoral support and ethical guidance to them as needed. This role is often described as being "a minister to ministers."

Until June of 2019 my Good Officer role largely entailed helping colleagues manage their conflicts with the congregations they served or with their ministerial colleagues. Then, in June of that same year, my life changed when this role took me on a sharp and unexpected turn that led me into direct conflict with the UUMA and soon thereafter the UUA.

As I was nearing the end of a four-month sabbatical, I became aware of a controversy that had erupted at the 2019 Spokane General Assembly, where the Rev. Dr. Todd Eklof, the General Assembly hosting minister from the UU Church of Spokane, had distributed his book *The*

Gadfly Papers: Three Inconvenient Essays by One Pesky Minister. The reaction was swift and severe. He was barred from further participation at General Assembly and interrogated by General Assembly and UUA officials. The reason these actions were taken was that the UUMA People of Color and Indigenous Chapter accused him of disseminating "racism, ableism, and the affirmation of other forms of oppression, including classism and homo-and transphobia."[56] It is important to note that not a single passage from *The Gadfly Papers* was cited to substantiate these serious allegations. [*Editor's note: That's because, as far as I've been able to discern, there was no such passage anywhere in the book.*] The attack on Todd continued with more unsubstantiated charges delivered in a harshly worded letter signed by 500 White UU ministers condemning the book, although many signees had not read the book. All of this had happened in a matter of days.

Since Rev. Eklof and I were both members of the same UUMA Chapter, I immediately reached out to him to offer Good Officer support. For some time, Todd and I had been discussing our mutual concerns about illiberal and intolerant trends in our religious movement expressed by our UU leadership. I knew Todd was raising important issues that warranted the attention of Unitarian Universalists. Before the publication of *The Gadfly Papers*, Todd asked for my feedback on an essay he had written describing how the skillful use of the ancient philosophical tool of logic could provide an effective, impartial way for Unitarian Universalists to examine and resolve controversies that had erupted in our movement. (This essay would become the third chapter of his book.) His essay was intellectually challenging and illuminating and convinced me that logic could be a useful tool to help to resolve conflicts. Indeed, Buddhist philosophy also uses logical reasoning to diagnose the ills that beset our minds. Islamic civilization cherished and preserved the tradition of Aristotelian logic when Western European civilization was mired in religious dogmatism. Ancient Indian, Chinese, and Greek civilizations all developed sophisticated systems of logic. These historic references to the reverence for logic deserve mention here inasmuch as the White ministers who condemned Todd's book dismissed the use of logic and reason as merely "the foundational stones of White Supremacy Culture."[57]

Ideological Dismissal of Logic

A UU clerical pronouncement abjuring the use of reason and logic is an alarming development in our liberal religious movement, which has historically championed the full use of our intellects in our religious explorations. This dismissal of logic and reason is another instance of how the ideas of Critical Race Theory have come to influence the thinking of our UU leadership. Critical Race Theory seeks to discredit and dismantle the epistemological foundations of our liberal religious tradition.

When I saw that Todd was being treated with such cruelty and contempt simply for sharing his honest views, I was shocked and dismayed. This bullying behavior reminded me of a playground pile-on! Yet I also came to a realization: I loved Todd, my brother in our chosen profession and liberal faith, admired his courage, and felt called to protect the freedom he was responsibly exercising. Until that moment I was not aware how much of a role love can play in helping us overcome our fears. Earlier I had realized that UUA leadership was imposing an illiberal, intolerant, divisive ideology upon us, yet I was afraid of speaking up lest I be publicly condemned. Now love liberated me from those fears. Todd is a kind, generous and wise minister who offered his book to call attention to alarming trends in our movement. He, too, feared a negative reaction but realized he would lose his self-respect if he did not summon the moral courage to share what he had written. He intended to initiate a much-needed honest dialogue among UUs concerning conflicts and controversies that are adversely affecting Unitarian Universalism today.[158]

The Price of Speaking Up

Todd was quickly censured and dis-fellowshipped by the UUMA and UUA leadership.[159] Such punitive actions serve as an effective control mechanism. If you can make people afraid, you can control them. It's a frightening time for many today who feel as though the slightest innocent slip can result in the loss of their livelihood and reputation. Fearing this, people feel wary, stifled, unsettled, and uncertain of what they can and cannot say.

The administrative tools to instill fear, couched in less threatening terms such as accountability, right relations, and beloved community, are now found in official UUMA policies. In the summer of 2020, the UUMA adopted institutional changes that created an opaque authoritarian leadership structure that has the power to censure ministers for unknown reasons. It's truly Kafkaesque. UU ministers now know that if they voice dissenting views, the response will be swift and the consequences severe, placing their livelihood and their reputation at stake. The clear message is that you'd better toe the party line!

Think for a moment of the harm inflicted on Todd that will affect him throughout his life by the actions taken by UU religious leaders. Since senior UU leadership has condemned Todd as someone who traffics in racist, classist, ableist, homophobic, and transphobic views, there are many UUs who know nothing at all about Todd and who will accept this verdict of Todd's character and spread those false pronouncements. In the minds of many UUs who don't know him, it is now okay to malign him as a stooge of the alt-right. It is profoundly disturbing when UU religious leaders resort to character assassination as a means of enforcing ideological conformity.

This public shaming and humiliation of Rev. Eklof was so hurriedly executed that you cannot help but wonder, when did the UUA and UUMA lose sight of his humanity, his inherent worth and dignity? I offer that our UU leadership, with their embrace of the soul-deadening social ideology of Critical Race Theory, merely saw Todd as a vehicle through which to flex their power to "decenter" a voice. They did not recognize Todd as an individual but only as a member of an identity group, a White man.

Sadly, the Critical Race Theory ideologues in the UUA leadership and the UUMA have lost sight of love in their treatment of Rev. Eklof. When he was censured by the UUMA Board there was no forewarning, no semblance of due process, nor was there any acknowledgment that 500 UU clergy had violated, *en masse*, our UUMA Guidelines, which expressly state, "I will not speak scornfully or in derogation of any colleague in public. In any private conversation concerning a colleague, I will speak responsibly and temperately. I will not solicit or encourage negative comments about a colleague or their ministry." Such hypocrisy and abuse of power destroy trust and have been most disheartening to witness.

Religious Tyranny

UUs have learned through painful historical experience that those who enforce dogmas and ideologies practice religious tyranny, and we want no part of that. Our hard-won freedom of conscience and expression is an essential religious right. We do not have dogmas or creeds but a covenant, a promise to dwell together in love as a theologically diverse religious body. Imposing beliefs upon another is a violation of a person's inner sanctum, wherein they alone have the right to listen to the voice of their own conscience and decide what is true, what is good and loving, what is beautiful, and what is sacred. Having freedom in our inner sanctums is necessary for true moral and spiritual discernment. That freedom lies at the heart of our liberal faith. In championing this inviolable freedom, we affirm our individuality, which enables each of us to make our unique contributions to the vast mosaic of life. Let me be clear: Individuality should not be confused or conflated with individualism, which asserts the supremacy of the isolated self.

Let me be clear on another point as well. Our freedom to our inner sanctum, our free and responsible search for truth and meaning is threatened by this new UU orthodoxy. There is clear evidence that our Fourth Principle is being targeted by UU leadership with an intent to constrain our freedom by adding an accountability clause.[160]

Cult of Certitude

When ideological views are imposed upon UUs it precludes the possibility of the free exchange of ideas and opinions necessary for a healthy denomination. The speed and the totality of the action taken against Rev. Eklof and the curtailing of debate about his book was not a reaction by rogue ministers or an overly aggressive advocacy group but an intentional action by our UU leadership. Rev. Eklof was not granted an honest hearing and was peremptorily condemned because his views ran counter to the new UU orthodoxy, which was on ample display in the Commission on Institutional Change report, *Widening the Circle of Concern*. Todd's show trial was over before it began; he was guilty of standing in the way of ideologues with their arrogant certitude. As James Baldwin, an African American playwright, poet, and activist

189

warned, "No one is more dangerous than he who imagines himself pure in heart; for his purity, by definition, is unassailable." Those possessed by ideological certitude feel empowered to overrule deliberative due process since they imagine themselves to be unassailably pure and infallibly correct. Thus, Todd was deemed an enemy of the UU state and had to be banished before his heresies spread. Now he has been airbrushed out of the collective image of UU ministers—disappeared, even as his book was thrown into trash bins by UU clergy at the General Assembly in Spokane, their variation of a book burning.

Broader Implications

Consider the broader implications of the official censuring and dis-fellowshipping of Rev. Eklof. My fellow UU clergy and our religious leaders also condemn UUs who share Todd's views. Yet most online reviews of *The Gadfly Papers* by Unitarian Universalists are glowing and appreciative. Then, too, the congregation I serve in Salem independently studied Rev. Eklof's book and concluded that the harsh accusations leveled against it were unsubstantiated. It surprised me that these members took this matter so seriously, but I have found it immensely heartening that they voted in a congregational meeting to protest the unjust treatment of Rev. Eklof to the UUA and the UUMA. Undoubtedly, there are thousands of Unitarian Universalists who agree in broad principle with the concerns raised by Rev. Eklof in his book. Which begs some questions: Do the clergy who harshly condemned him also condemn UUs who share his concerns? Who gave UU clergy such censorious powers in our free-faith tradition in the first place? These questions take on a more ominous gravity since our UU leadership has declared that they have a theological mandate to press forward on changes to UUism and our Seven Principles based on their own self-declaration of the alleged complicity of UUism with white supremacy. We have never been on the eve of darker days for UUism than we are now.

Consider what is now happening in our purportedly democratic, non-creedal religious Association. There is a growing constriction upon the spiritual and intellectual freedom of the ministry and the laity. Religious authority, the UUA Board of Trustees and UUMA, is acting like a boa constrictor that squeezes its captured prey ever tighter. In the many recurring instances where such constrictions upon freedom occur, history teaches us that the longer you wait to cry out in protest, the less lung capacity and courage there is to do so.

Recognizing this constricting threat has led me to recognize my deep appreciation for our heretical, free-faith tradition. I draw particular inspiration from forebears in our dual tradition who have been truth's courageous emissaries and love's compassionate embodiments in our hurting, unjust world. This love motivates me to speak out to protect our religious body as best I can. Ours is, at its best, a living, evolving religious tradition that invites us to be our authentic selves, to grow spiritually with others, to create a loving community that we might walk the paths of compassion and gratitude, meaning, and purpose. My rich experience with congregations has shown me that our free faith tradition is worth protecting against a hijacking by illiberal, ideological forces that brook no dissent.

My Own Road

It is my responsibility, as a UU minister entrusted with a free pulpit by the congregation I am honored to serve, to speak the truth as best I can regarding matters important to us all. Certainly, the spiritual health and vitality of our religious tradition are of primary concern to all UUs, and thus I will continue to speak out to preserve this as I am able.

My public support of Rev. Eklof led to some uncomfortable encounters with UUMA leadership. I was advised to back off—told that my role as a Good Officer was to bring Todd to heel, never mind that the UUMA was, in my view, the transgressing party. As though to prove this point, the UUMA Board unilaterally censured him without following the due processes prescribed in the UUMA Guidelines for Professional Conduct, acting in direct violation of their own guidelines! At the same time, they countenanced the harsh and intemperate letter signed by 500 White colleagues with their silence. Then, to add salt to his wounds, the UUA removed him from ministerial fellowship for, among other things, his "refusal to engage".[161] The fact is that the Ministerial Fellowship Committee (MFC) leaped at the opportunity to investigate him. Since the lead investigator had publicly gone on record condemning Rev. Eklof's book, I questioned the fairness of this proceeding. I was completely ignored, and Todd was promptly removed from UU ministerial fellowship. Next, the UUMA removed him from membership since you must be in fellowship to be a member.

I am happy to note here that the powers of the UUMA and UUA are not absolute. In our congregational polity, only congregations have the power to call and ordain ministers, and the UU Church of Spokane continues to have him serving them. The UUMA and the UUA cannot excommunicate him.

Not surprisingly, just as I was completing my fourth and final term as a Good Officer, I was removed from this position by UUMA Pacific Northwest Chapter leaders at the recommendation of the UUMA Board. Given all of that had transpired since June of 2019, I felt I had no choice but to join some other dissenting colleagues in resigning from the UUMA, an organization I do not trust and for which I have lost respect.

Compassion Litmus Test

A religious movement whose primary source of spiritual fuel is anger and resentment will not last. Fewer and fewer will, over time, want to be part of something that does not uplift and unify. Every religious movement should be required to pass religious scholar Karen Armstrong's "Litmus Test." Some religions manifest in life-affirming, liberating ways. Others are divisive, destructive, and oppressive. Sometimes, in the thick of life, it can be hard to tell the difference. You need to pay attention. Armstrong wisely notes that the litmus test for all religions should be the "Compassion Test." Concerning this she says:

> The one and only test of a valid religious idea, doctrinal statement, spiritual experience, or devotional practice was that it must lead directly to practical compassion.
>
> If your understanding of the divine made you kinder, more empathetic, and impelled you to express this sympathy in concrete acts of loving-kindness, this was good theology. But if your notion of God made you unkind, belligerent, cruel, or self-righteous, or if it led you to kill in God's name, it was bad theology.
>
> Compassion was the litmus test for the prophets of Israel, for the rabbis of the Talmud, for Jesus, for Paul, and for Muhammad, not to mention Confucius, Lao-Tzu, The Buddha, or the sages of the Upanishads.

Here's the question we must ask: What do you imagine would be the result of such a litmus test administered to Unitarian Universalists today? My hunch is that most UU congregations would score impressively high on the compassion scale. Yet higher up, at the leadership level of the UUA, I think the score would be much lower. I could not give the leadership of our movement a passing grade on compassion. In challenging moments they have failed to show it, nor do they encourage us to genuinely practice it. All the great religious traditions have, from time to time, gotten hijacked by zealots, ideologues, fundamentalists, and used as vehicles for divisive actions. You can read about this in the news almost any day, as religious fundamentalists and extremists of all stripes lead followers far away from the practices of compassion. It is naïve to believe that Unitarian Universalism is immune from such hijackings.

In all humility, every one of us is called to ask, "Does the way I am practicing my religion pass the litmus test of compassion?" All of us need to ask this question, "If you are consumed by hatred for your enemies, will you become an enemy to yourself?"

The lesson of history is clear that attempts to impose heaven on Earth through the ideological exercise of power don't lead to heaven—they lead to hell (on Earth). That is where the UUA and the UUMA are leading us. They may think they know where they are going, but their ideological blinders distort their vision. They think they see the mirage of a perfect society ahead, but a clearer vision shows it be a desert of tribal discord and division. They claim, and may honestly believe, that they occupy the moral high ground, but so have so many before who were so arrogant and self-righteous that they could not see the beam in their own eyes, even as they made it their business to remove the specks in others'.

When I assert that UUA and UUMA leadership is leading us to hell I am not speaking in anger or judgmentally, but with a sad awareness of what lies ahead of us on the path they are urging us to walk. It is a path without love and compassion, without understanding and forgiveness. It is a path of enforced conformity that entails the denial of freedom of conscience and expression. It is a path that will lead to more canceling, dis-fellowshipping, discord, mistrust, anger, fear, and oppression. This is nothing new—it's just a modern iteration of the ancient, oppressive practices of priestcraft in progressive guise.

When I was with Todd, I witnessed how the UUMA and the UUA put him through hell, censuring him and removing him from UUA Ministerial Fellowship. It was unjust, authoritarian, and cruel. This will be recorded as a dark moment in our movement's history.

11. UUMA Board to Ministers: Shut Up!

By Rev. Richard Trudeau

Prologue

Disagree and you're racist. This was the tacit but unmistakable message sent by UUA leaders at the 1997 General Assembly in Phoenix, where "Journey Toward Wholeness" (the predecessor of today's racial-justice effort - JTW for short) was up for consideration. The morning of the vote there was no debate; for hours the delegates heard one pro-JTW speaker after another, one of whom (a Black seminarian) went so far as to imply that a vote against JTW would amount to a vote in favor of a return to slavery. When the vote came, I stood to vote "no." (I was not willing to "confess" my "complicity in" institutional racism because "complicity in" connotes "responsibility for.") It was a terrifying experience—I was halfway back in a ballroom with 2,500 UUs, and no one in front of me was standing; I was afraid to turn around; my wife said a few others were standing further back. After the result was announced ("passed overwhelmingly") a white man I didn't know came up to me and said, "I want you to know that lots of us are uncomfortable with this, but we don't want to be seen as racist." A black man I didn't know came up to me and demanded I explain my vote. I told him I approved of the goal but was uncomfortable with the means.

UU World, Now and Then

UU World is the only mass communication vehicle we have in the denomination. It's ideally positioned to engage UUs in a debate regarding the direction of the denomination and other issues that require discussion. As difficult as the task may be to provide a public outlet for agreeing and dissenting voices, it is essential that the editorial board maintain a professional balance of the opinions published. Sadly, that balance has not been achieved.

Today, *UU World* is in the tank. It is unashamedly a propaganda organ for the current "dismantle our white supremacy culture" ideology. This has been the case for some time, but the editor's column in a recent issue (Winter 2019) makes it undeniable. Here are the first two paragraphs.

> Are you detecting changes in the UUA's communications, including *UU World*? In the Summer issue, I mentioned that the magazine was changing its editorial approach in response to the UUA's commitment to center voices on the margins and focus on becoming a truly multicultural, antiracist faith movement.

> The editors began moving in that direction in 2014, boosting the frequency and prominence of articles about racism in the United States. Since President Susan Frederick-Gray's election in 2017, however, all UUA staff groups have been charged to examine how their work has privileged culturally dominant groups and perpetuated white supremacy culture. The administration has given the magazine and other

UUA communications teams—especially the UUA website and its social media channels—a mandate to prioritize and serve historically marginalized people working to undo the legacy of white supremacy culture in the UUA and beyond.

This shift in editorial emphasis may indeed have a wider objective in mind, but it appears the shift is both a departure from and at the expense of an earlier editorial position. Twenty years ago, *UU World* (then called simply *World*) was allowed to at least occasionally publish articles that dissented from UU leadership policies and positions.

Below is an article I wrote for a 2000 issue of *UU World*. Re-reading it now, it seems to me that Critical Race Theory must have underlain the official UU racial-justice ideology even then, though at the time I had never heard anyone mention it. (For an introduction to Critical Race Theory, see Mel Pine's blog "The UU Crisis, Explained."[162] For analysis and refutation, see Daniel Subotnik's "What's Wrong with Critical Race Theory: Reopening the Case for Middle Class Values."[163])

My Racialization, by Richard Trudeau

UU World, March/April 2000

I'm white. In 1951, as I was about to enter first grade, my mother said, "There may be Negro children at school. Other children may call them '[N-word].' Don't ever say that. It hurts people's feelings!" I was puzzled. Why would some children want to hurt other children's feelings? "Because," my mother explained, "some people don't think

Negroes are as good as other people." "Is that true?" I asked. "Of course not," she said.

Thus, I learned about racism. The lesson continued through the 1950s and 1960s, as the civil rights movement unfolded on TV. I saw the firehoses and the dogs. And I felt: Racists are slimeballs. Even when I learned about more subtle forms of racism, that feeling never left me.

I, therefore, find it hard to keep listening to some in the UUA leadership when they solemnly assure me that, as a white, I can't help but be some kind of racist. The term "racist," no matter how prefixed with modifiers (like "institutional"), still feels like an insult. It's as if they're telling me, "Richard, we have a more advanced understanding of what it means to be a slimeball, and we've concluded that, in this more nuanced sense, you, Richard, are a slimeball."

But there was more to that conversation with my parents back in 1951. If there might be Negroes in school, I asked, where did they live? Why had I never seen any? My father said, "They stick with their own kind." That meant, of course, that we whites were also a kind, and that we stuck with our kind, too—though that was never said. (One of the rules of being white is that you never talk about it, except by indirection.) My father was teaching me about racial boundaries, and that it was important to respect them. I was being racialized.

My racialization has handicapped me all my life. Fifty years later, it still affects me. Whenever I'm getting to know a person of another race, for instance, I notice an extra awkwardness. I feel a conflict within me—between what I learned at age five (racial categories are important) and what I believe now (racial categories are meaningless).

If the UUA leadership would like to help me, they can stop calling me a rarefied racist and advise me instead on how to deal with my racialization. (How can I minimize its effects? How can I avoid transmitting it to younger people?) That, it seems to me, would also promote the UUA's announced goal of "dismantling racism."

Racialization is the more fundamental evil, in that it makes racism possible. Eliminate racialization, and racism, in all its forms, will evaporate. (end of the article)

Fulfilling the Promise

At the 1999 Salt Lake City General Assembly, the chair of the UUA Fulfilling the Promise Committee addressed the 2,000 delegates, as did representatives from UU congregations who also took to the stage to share their stories in a "riveting program written for the Fulfilling the Promise Committee." Fulfilling the Promise was a four-year effort by UU leadership to examine UU covenants. The details of the program are not as important as its central purpose, which was (in my opinion) to persuade congregations to agree that it was okay with them that moving forward the UUA would call the shots on social-justice priorities. The initiative sank like a stone when congregational conversations led by appointed facilitators met with resounding rejection.

I believe the UUA's experience with Fulfilling the Promise is an important reason why today the "dismantle our white supremacy culture" ideology is being imposed top-down. National leaders at the UUA, in our seminaries, and in the UU Ministers' Association learned not to ask for congregational input.

More recently the UUA Board declared that the UUA is an anti-racist, anti-oppression, and multicultural organization (or words to that effect—ARAOMC for short). This has encouraged many UU social justice activists to conclude that ARAOMC work was now mandated to constitute the principal focus of every congregation's life. I don't think that's what the board intended, or—if I'm wrong and it is what they intended—I don't think they had the right to mandate any such thing. The UUA is the creation of its congregations and exists to serve them (primarily by certifying ministers, creating RE curricula, and publicizing UUism), not to lead them.

Censured

In the Spring of 2018, I received a letter of censure from the Board of Trustees of the UU Ministers' Association. For some time, I had been posting to the UU ministers' group ("UUMA Colleagues") on Facebook and speaking at UUMA chapter meetings about my concerns with the UU racial justice orthodoxy. The precipitating event seems to have been the following post (March 2018).

> A PLACE TO DISCUSS? I have reservations about current UU racial justice ideology and would like to find a place to discuss them with colleagues (of all races). I can't imagine that our moderators would

allow such a discussion here. Can anyone suggest a place?

Not intending to discuss my reservations now, but so readers will know the kind of thing I'm talking about, here are brief statements of some of them:

> We use a non-standard definition of "racism" (racial prejudice + power) that, while emphasizing the crucial factor of relative power, tends to make anti-white racial prejudice invisible.

> Some UU people of color who are not African American, whose ethnic group has not suffered anything like what African Americans have suffered, appear to be appropriating the moral authority of African Americans.

> Much of our eagerness to attract African Americans to our congregations seems motivated by white guilt.

> The Commission on Institutional Change has called on congregations (2/10/18) to "answer the call to fund BLUU [Black Lives of Unitarian Universalism] as an act of reparation for the denial of opportunities over centuries." As someone who in 1969 was present at a demonstration at the headquarters of the NY Catholic archdiocese demanding that such "reparation" be paid to African American organizations, and who later decided it was a terrible idea, alarm bells are going off in my head.

The letter of censure was sent to me and six other people—the Executive Committee and Good Officers of my chapter of the UUMA. It said that the UUMA Board was taking this action "as a result of complaints made against you on Facebook and in your chapter meetings. We hope that in receiving this admonishment from your fellow ministers you may take time to reflect upon how your words have been harmful to colleagues . . ." I understand the UUMA Board's claim to be that my questioning had caused "harm" to UU ministers of color—though no minister of color, or white minister for that matter, had ever expressed to me any such thing.

In response, I eventually wrote three letters to the UUMA Board. In the third, sent five months after receiving the letter of censure, and frustrated that the first two had not been responded to or even acknowledged, I told them that their letter of censure undercuts a foundational Unitarian Universalist value, *viz.*: each person's right to ask questions. This value is what historically distinguished the Unitarian and Universalist denominations from other sects and enabled them eventually to combine. It is not an aspect of "white supremacy culture." It is not an aspect of UU culture that is transient—to use Theodore Parker's terms—but an aspect that is permanent. It is non-negotiable. If it is compromised, we cease to be who we are.

The right to ask questions is our version of U.S. civil society's "freedom of speech" and just as the purpose of the latter is not to protect speech that is popular or approved by national leaders—such speech needs no protection—the purpose of the right to ask questions in UUism is not to protect questions that are popular or approved by denominational leaders.

By its letter of censure, the board has sided with the vocal people on Facebook who choose to interpret every questioning of their ideas as a personal attack that justifies the silencing and ostracism of the questioner.

The UU movement is losing its way! It needs its national leaders, perhaps as never before. In particular, the UU movement needs the UUMA Board to help guide it back onto the right path. Instead, by attacking one of UUism's foundational values, the board is leading the UU movement further astray.

This letter also received no acknowledgment or response.

Todd Eklof Censured

In August 2019, the UUMA Board of Trustees sent Todd Eklof a letter of censure which, unlike mine, was also sent to the approximately 1,700 members of the UUMA. Six months later, in November 2019, a letter signed by more than sixty UUMA members (including me) was sent to the UUMA Board protesting their action. It said, in part,

> We believe your actions violate our freedom of the pulpit, a freedom we believe extends to our writings. Those who initiated this letter find no violation of our covenant in Todd's book, only ideas which challenge particular approaches to anti-oppression currently in favor with many colleagues. All signatories believe that the changes you are making to our norms of ministerial collegiality and freedom of the pulpit are creating a deep divide amongst UUs and are resulting in an atmosphere of fear and distrust.

The UUMA Board responded to this letter on November 25. Its response to the above charge boiled down to this: "We, too, value the free pulpit. However . . . With freedom comes responsibility."

Free Thought and Expression

The preamble to our Seven Principles reads, "We, the member congregations of the Unitarian Universalist Association, covenant to affirm and promote . . . Our Fourth Principle, a free and responsible search for truth and meaning . . ." This principle grants us both the gift and burden to continually examine either our personal or collective theological or religious precepts. The Fifth Principle begins by affirming and promoting "the right of conscience . . ."

To younger UUs, the Seven Principles have always been there, and younger UUs consequently tend to think that here is the basis for the UU commitment to free thought and expression. However, we are seeing a disturbing trend. UU leaders, in particular the UUMA Board, claim to have a superior understanding of what is "responsible."

Our Seven Principles were written in the mid-1980s but reflect values from our heritage denominations. At their American beginnings in the early 1800s, Unitarians spoke of "the right of private judgment." Even earlier, in the late 1700s, American Universalists spoke of the "soul of liberty." Both groups were referring to the right of free thought and expression. And while it was well understood that not all speech is proper—famously, one cannot shout "Fire!" in a crowded theater—our founders thought it best not to include a qualifier, like "responsible," that could be used to stifle speech.

Ministers of my generation—in seminary 30 years ago—were required by the UUA to learn about Unitarian history from *A History of Unitarianism* by Earl Morse Wilbur (Harvard University Press, third edition 1947), which held that the essence of Unitarianism was freedom, reason, and tolerance. By freedom Wilbur meant the absolute right of each person to decide religious matters for themselves; by reason, the use of reason in religious discourse; and by tolerance, tolerance of those with differing points of view. The Universalists held those values too. In their censure of Todd Eklof, the UUMA Board has violated all three! According to my training, therefore, these national "leaders" have left the denomination.

Will Rogers said, "If you're ridin' ahead of the herd, take a look back every now and then to make sure it's still there." While the UUMA Board may have succeeded in intimidating most of our ministers, I hope that soon the UUMA Board will look back and see that the important people—the people in the pews—are not following.

12. Accusation and Polarization I

*It all started on June 20, 2017 when Rev. R.V.
Rowan received an email from a Unitarian
Universalist Ministers' Association Good Officer.*

This chapter recounts a story of an early instance of the overreach we are now more commonly witnessing as our UU leadership moves to expand its authoritarian concept of accountability across UUism. This is a true story involving three Unitarian Universalist ministers. We at the Fifth Principle Project were given access to original source materials by the minister who was accused of views that could have led to disciplinary action by the Unitarian Universalist Ministers' Association (UUMA). The UUMA is a professional association of ministers who are in fellowship with the UUA. Membership in this professional association is voluntary. Actual names have been changed to protect the privacy and avoid possible recriminations for the parties involved.

Dramatis Personae

- Rev. R.V. Rowan: accused minister.
- Rev. M.J. Goodwright: UUMA Good Officer.

- Rev. J.V. Acosta: accusing minister.

The Scene

- A community event presentation by Rev. Rowan in the city where Rev. Acosta's church is located.

The story begins on June 20, 2017, when Rev. R.V. Rowan received an unexpected email from Rev. M.J. Goodwright acting in the capacity of a UUMA Good Officer. A Good Officer advocates for UU ministers, offering pastoral support and ethical guidance as required. Rev. Rowan, who is not a member of the UUMA, was completely unaware of any action pending before that professional association that would require the assignment of a Good Officer.

The Accusation Email

From: Rev. M.J. Goodwright, Good Officer
To: Rev. R.V. Rowan

Rev. R.V. Rowan,

I am the minister at the UU Church of (name withheld), but today I am writing in my capacity as a Good Officer in our district. I would like to arrange a time to meet with you and Rev. J.V. Acosta, First Parish in (name withheld).

Rev. J.V. Acosta has received complaints about your presentation at a community event at (name withheld) to discuss police brutality. Rev. Acosta's parish has been working very hard on anti-racism initiatives and also in building bridges with marginalized communities in (city).

If what Rev. Acosta heard is true, your message seemed in contradiction to the work Rev. Acosta's church has been doing and incongruous with UU work nationwide. (I understand you were speaking as a chaplain, but, nonetheless, you are also identified as a UU minister.)

If, on the other hand, what Rev. Acosta has heard is untrue, you need a chance to tell what happened from your viewpoint. In either case, I feel it is important to clear up any misunderstandings and also to clarify for ourselves and each other what the boundary issues are in such a presentation. Would you please contact me so that we can arrange a time to meet? (phone number)

Thank you, Rev. M.J. Goodwright, Good Officer

Unpacking the Accusation Email

There are two immediate observations about the email received by Rev. Rowan. The first observation is that Rev. Rowan was speaking at a community event and not at Rev. Acosta's church. The question raised here is what exactly is the jurisdiction of the UUMA over conversations covered by its oversight? This question of jurisdiction is important, since without delineation of boundaries even overheard conversations at a local coffee shop could well be deemed as within the jurisdiction of the UUMA!

The second observation is that the accusing minister, Rev. Acosta, was not present at the community event. From the email, the only information known is that an anonymous third party was dissatisfied with Rev. Rowan's opinions expressed at the community event and later complained to Rev. Acosta. "Rev. J.V. Acosta has received complaints about your presentation at a community event . . ."

In many ways, it appears that UUism has lost its commonsense compass. There once was a time when if someone disagreed with another's opinion, they would speak up themselves and initiate a one-on-one conversation. The covenant of many UU congregations includes social norms such as listening respectfully and talking directly with one another to resolve conflicts. Yet in the new UUism, there is a new social norm that disregards the corrosive damage that can be done to a person personally and professionally when formal charges are initiated by a professional organization based solely on an anonymous, unverified third-party account.

The Reply to the Accusation Email

Rev. Rowan responded to the accusation email received from Rev. Goodwright, the Good Officer, and appropriately included the accusing minister, Rev. Acosta, in the email conversation. This response provided factual information missing from the original accusation email, noting, for example, that the presentation in question was not on police brutality. Rev. Rowan rightly questioned why direct one-on-one dialogue was not used to resolve the conflict and why the preferred action taken by the accuser was to file a complaint with a representative from an organization of which Rev. Rowan was not a member. In the closing paragraphs of the email, Rev. Rowan observes that the community event devolving into an experience that "was worse than useless." We shall learn more later about the dynamics of the community event that will shed some light on the source of the complaint leveled against Rev. Rowan. Rev. Rowan concludes the email with a willingness to engage in a one-on-one dialogue, "perhaps for lunch."

From: Rev. Rowan
To: Rev. Goodwright
CC: Rev. Acosta

Dear Rev. Goodwright,

At the moment, I am in (location) County, assisting bereaved family members and (others) searching for bodies after a triple drowning. In the past four weeks, I have responded as a chaplain to (accident) fatalities, the drowning of a 14-year-old, a law enforcement use of deadly force, a suicide, the death of the 19 year old daughter of a State Trooper, an attempted domestic violence murder and a twenty year old police officer killed en route to rescue a drowning woman.

So, you'll forgive me if I'm a bit short in my response.

Since I do not know the nature of the complaints made, and since they were made neither to me personally nor even to you, I don't really see how you and I can address them, nor why we should. After all, neither Reverend Acosta nor you are my employer, so it seems unlikely that the complainant expected either of you to do something about me.

He, she or they are adults - by definition, if they attended a (event name) - and thus quite capable of bringing their concerns directly to me. (State) is a small state. I am not difficult to find.

Moreover, Unitarian Universalism is a non-dogmatic faith. In the unlikely event that somehow, in my free and responsible search for truth and meaning, I happened to arrive at a message that is "in contradiction to the work Rev. Acosta's church has been doing and incongruous with UU work nationwide" that would not mean that a boundary had been crossed, only that a UU was being . . . well, a UU. Perhaps Rev. Acosta could explain this to his/her/they congregants?

In any case, you were apparently misinformed as to the subject of the event. It was not "police brutality" but (subject of event), as you will see if you take a moment to peruse the website. (A link was provided.)

My specific assignment for the panel was to talk about the emotional challenges of policing, the only area in which I can claim some expertise. As requested by the organizers, I described the work I do, and the effects that exposure to trauma has on (certain groups in the state), and what we do here in (our State) to mitigate those effects.

I have been a panelist and an invited speaker speaking on the same subject in the same terms all over the country to diverse audiences from various disciplines including clergy, medical, law, theology/divinity and college students and graduates, physicians and surgeons, the FBI National Academy, hospital and prison chaplains, incarcerated persons and not a few Unitarian Universalists. Up until now, the UUA has been reasonably pleased to claim me as a UU minister and has even honored me for exactly the work I described at the (named event.)

As you pointed out, I was speaking as a chaplain, but I am an ordained UU minister. I am very sorry indeed if you feel it somehow harms the reputation of (State) Unitarian Universalist ministers to be publicly associated with someone who responds to sudden, violent deaths, comforts the bereaved (no matter who they are) and seeks to maintain the well-being of (our State's) splendid (named state) law enforcement officials.

Though I am grateful for your concern, I feel no need of a chance to tell you or Rev. Acosta what happened from my viewpoint. My viewpoint is that the event was worse than useless, but not because earnest, well-meaning people like me were naive enough to agree to participate. As soon as I have a moment, I plan to discuss my views with the board of the (State) Humanities Council, but as it had nothing to do with the UU Church in (City) or (City) or anywhere else, I don't see any reason why you need concern yourself about it further.

Unless, of course, you were intending to extend your collegial sympathy and support for my having endured a needlessly unpleasant experience smack in the middle of a month that was tragic and difficult even by chaplain standards? If so, thank you so much. And naturally, I would be delighted to meet any time - perhaps for lunch? - with my colleagues in the UU ministry.

Yours in faith,

Rev. Rowan

Unpacking the Reply to Accusation Email

Rev. Rowan's reply email speaks for itself. It introduced facts into the conversation, questioned the jurisdiction of the Rev. Goodwright's UUMA Good Office, and indicated that there was shared dissatisfaction with the community event. Nonetheless, Rev. Rowan is willing to move to a resolution by having one-on-one conversations. A rationale is offered below why Rev. Goodwright, in the capacity as a UUMA Good Officer, may have agreed initially to become involved. The Code of Conduct of the UUMA in effect at this time indicates that:

> In most instances, a member who believes a colleague's behavior to be inconsistent with the Code of Conduct should express their concern directly. As an alternative, or should the direct approach not achieve the desired result, a Chapter Good Offices Person (GOP) should be consulted. A GOP is initially neutral, advising the member, and exploring the possibility of an informal resolution of the concern.

Once it was established, however, that Rev. Rowan was not a member of the UUMA, it would have been prudent for Rev. Goodwright to step aside since there was no administrative or professional association authority to be engaged. We will see that was not to be the case. Not only was there a lack of jurisdictional authority, a review of the Code of Conduct rules of the UUMA at the time reveals that simply disagreeing with or failing to understand a minister's presentation is not grounds for action. We cannot dismiss, however, larger events consuming UUism in the summer of 2017. In April 2017, UUism had become deeply embroiled in controversy by the declaration by the UUA Board of UUism's complicity with white supremacy. Charges of harm or misconduct were just entering their cottage industry phase when accusations could become actionable regardless of any factual basis.

Not a UUMA Member

The reply email by Rev. Goodwright is unfortunate in that after having learned that Rev. Rowan was not a UUMA member, a UUMA Good Officer, therefore, having no authority to intervene, Rev. Goodwright nonetheless persisted. We have come to see over the three years since this event that there is an ever-growing appetite by UU leadership to extend authority beyond established boundaries. In 2020, through the report from the Commission on Institutional Change, our UU leadership granted itself a theological mandate to empower an official action to abandon our liberal values and begin a process to change our Seven Principles.

From: Rev. Goodwright, Good Officer
To: Rev. Rowan

Rev. Rowan,

That my request struck a nerve is obvious, because your response is so very defensive. I am sorry. Further I am sorry for the stressful and sad last few weeks you have gone through. Good Lord! I won't list my own challenges in that same time frame, but simply reflect that ministry –

whether as chaplain or parish minister – is hard work and sometimes heartbreaking work, too. More is expected of us than even seems possible to give sometimes, and yet we still are called to put ourselves in the path of tragedy and grief. That's why our relationships with colleagues are so important.

I think you misunderstood the reason for my request to meet. As you are not a member of the UU Ministers Association, perhaps you are unaware of the Good Officer program or its purpose.

The UUMA's Good Officers Handbook says:

It is the responsibility of the Good Officer to incarnate collegiality in the concrete situations where the living tradition of the liberal ministry is at stake.

- The Good Officer helps ministers when we're in tension with each other.
- The Good Officer helps ministers when we're in tension with the institutions we serve.
- The Good Officer helps ministers when we're in tension with the Unitarian Universalist Association.

In this case, the first example applies: You and Rev. Acosta are in tension with one another. My role is to help the two of you set that relationship to rights again. My role is not as accuser or judge, but as mediator, trying to help ministers - colleagues - repair relationships with one another or with the institutions they serve. Rev. Acosta asked me to help with that, so I reached out to you, as my role as Good Officer dictates.

Perhaps that seems an odd thing to say, that you and Rev. Acosta are in tension with one another. But, when a UU minister – even unwittingly and unintentionally – undermines the work of another, that makes for broken relationships. Rev. Acosta is the minister in (City).

Whether rightly or wrongly, (Rev. Acosta's congregation) feels your presentation at (event) has had a negative impact on their social justice ministry, particularly their Black Lives Matter ministry – and thus Rev. Acosta's ministry as well. I know you didn't intend that outcome. But

Rev. Acosta has to keep on serving in (City) after you dropped in for a few hours and then left.

The boundary issue in question has nothing to do with what you or (he/she/they) or I or anyone believes, but with impinging on the work of the parish in whose city you were presenting that night. They feel (again, rightly or wrongly) they are left holding pieces of something they have been working hard to build.

What is hoped for in a situation where one inadvertently hurts a UU parish or the ministry of a colleague is an attempt to make things right again. I have never questioned the fact that you are a UU minister. But, because you are not in fellowship with the UUA, you are thus not a signatory to the UUMA covenant that guides the relationships of UU ministers. Nonetheless, because you are a UU minister, I am asking for a meeting with you and Rev. Acosta to work to repair what has been broken. That's all. I don't mean to make it seem simple because it isn't. But, truly, keeping good relationships with our colleagues is critical in a profession that is often lonely and heartbreaking, as you know so well.

Thank you,

Rev. Goodwright, Good Officer

I Have a Complaint Too

In Rev. Rowan's response to Rev. Goodwright, we see the negative impact of the new UUism that shuns debate. Rather, in the new UUism speech and language are to be monitored for harm. Accordingly, speakers can, and should, be barred from the podium if opinions are not in alignment with UU liberatory theology or because someone simply doesn't like what they hear.

It appears the dynamics at the community event that was earlier characterized by Rev. Rowan as "worse than useless" fits the model where speech deemed harmful can be shouted down. Rev. Rowan even wondered if members of Rev. Acosta's congregation were among those "who displayed aggressive incivility and insensitivity toward me and other participants . . ." If such was the case, "It could even be that Rev. Acosta's actions are impinging on my ministry far more than the reverse." This interaction is not headed for a good place.

From: Rev. Rowan
To: Rev. Goodwright, Good Officer

Reverend Goodwright,

I am not at all defensive, only perplexed.

I can't imagine how a description of my work could possibly impinge upon (name of Congregation) ministry let alone leave them "holding pieces of what they had been trying to build." My remarks presented information broadly available to Unitarian Universalists and, indeed, every citizen in (City) and beyond through my books, and various articles written about me (in, among other places, in the *UU World* and the (City newspaper).

Nor can I bring myself to believe that Rev. Acosta's ministry has been to persuade (his/her) congregants that looking after the needs of mourners (of all races, sexes, orientations and faiths) in the (State) and providing pastoral care to (profession) and other law enforcement officers (again of all races, sexes, orientations and faiths) is somehow antithetical to social justice.

However, if members of Rev. Acosta's UU congregation were among those few who displayed aggressive incivility and insensitivity toward me and other participants and ruined what would otherwise have been a fruitful and enlightening discussion of the (emotional challenges of policing and being policed), then there are indeed some serious boundary issues that need to be addressed. It could even be that Rev. Acosta's actions are impinging on my ministry far more than the reverse. After all, both Unitarian Universalists and members of "marginalized groups" have been known to get lost in the woods.

In that case, we should certainly meet. Rashly assuming no new tragedies that require my presence, I should be available to meet next week, perhaps on Thursday or Friday (29, 30)?

One last thing: far from "dropping in for a few hours," I, too, must keep on serving in (City) as I have in (City) and (City) and everywhere in between for the past sixteen years. The (agency name) is a statewide agency.

Pax,

Rev. Rowan

Good Officer Recognizes Complexity of Situation

Rev. Goodwright, the Good Officer, now recognizes the complexity of the situation with all parties claiming a charge of harm. No longer is the Good Officer calling upon an accused minister to account for their actions, but suggesting rather that, "A face-to-face meeting would work better."

From: Rev. Goodwright
To: Rev. Rowan, Rev. Acosta

Dear Rev. Rowan and Rev. Acosta,

I am back now. Pretty exhausted, but back.

I am not sure where we stand with Rev. Rowan's request for information on what the problem is. Rev. Rowan, this is my understanding: Rev. Acosta received reports from her local SURJ (Showing up for Racial Justice) chapter that your remarks were inflammatory to people of color in the audience that night. I also hear, Rev. Rowan, that the event was upsetting to you, and that you felt attacked. That's it in a nutshell, from my understanding. Rev. Rowan and Rev. Acosta, you can both correct my verbiage if I am stating your viewpoints or experiences inaccurately, but I am hoping we don't get into a long email conversation about this. Because the issue is sensitive on both sides, my feeling is that email won't help. A face-to-face meeting would work better.

Thank you both so much.

All best,

Rev. Goodwright, Good Officer

Black Lives Matters Team Has Letter

From: Rev. Acosta
To: Rev. Goodwright, Rev. Rowan

Hi Rev. Goodwright and Rev. Rowan,

I was out of town at General Assembly all week last week. Just arrived home yesterday.

Rev. Goodwright is correct in her statements. The Black Lives Matter Team at (Congregation) has written a letter they would like me to share with Rev. Rowan regarding the event.

Rev. Rowan, would you like me to email the letter before our meeting, or would like me to bring it to the meeting?

My plan is to meet at the (Congregation) on Friday morning.

Blessings,

Rev. Acosta

Black Lives Matter Team Letter

The next day, Rev. Rowan received the letter from the Black Lives Matter Team.

LETTER (Undated): Dear Rev. Rowan,

As advocates for racial justice at (Congregation, City), we are concerned about your words and actions surrounding the (name and date of the event). It is our hope in reaching out personally that we might find connection and understanding that will bring healing.

We understand you were invited as a panelist to speak about the emotional harm of policing on law enforcement and the community. We acknowledge the importance of the ministry you do as a (State Office) chaplain. We see that your personal and professional connections with law enforcement officers give you a unique understanding of the physical dangers and emotional trauma experienced by officers in the line of duty and off duty.

We feel concern that you misread the crowd that evening in your remarks and attitude towards audience speakers. That created harm to an audience that was a majority people of color. When a person of color in the audience asked you for recognition of the emotional harm done to her community by repeated negative interactions with police, your words failed to convey that recognition and the compassion that would have been validating and healing. We trust that as a Unitarian Universalist, you believe in the values of justice, equity and compassion in relationships. We understand our first and second UU principles to mean that, especially in public settings, white people should listen and trust people of color when harm is being named.

Tragic and unjust behavior by local law enforcement toward people of color has made the headlines in our city over the last year. (City) experienced the shooting death of (two named individuals), a young black man, by a white police officer in March. Last summer, the county jail released to the media photographs of black, Muslim women without head coverings who were arrested at a Black Lives Matter protest. These women were also given more charges by prosecutors than white arrestees for the same protest. It is against this background of very public physical and emotional harm to communities of color in (City) that the (Title) event happened.

When we learned about your appearance at the event from attendees, we then discovered your public post about the event on the website (name of website). Your post clearly indicates that the event was upsetting to you. We are alarmed that in your post and subsequent comments, your words turned from defensive to hostile. In the comments, you demeaned people of color at the event and personally insulted the panel moderator's race, religion and profession. This is unacceptable, particularly from a minister representing our faith.

We ask you to re-examine your words and learn from them more about white fragility – the tendency of white people to become defensive when exposed to racial stress. We invite you to be in dialogue with us towards taking responsibility for these actions and the harm they caused and making steps to repair and mend the relationships affected. We ask you to make a public commitment to do better.

Sincerely,

Black Lives Matter Team (Congregation and city)

June 28th, 2017

Accused of Something by Somebody

From: Rev. Rowan
To: Rev. Goodwright, Rev. Acosta

Dear Rev. Goodwright and Rev. Acosta,

So let me get this straight: the original plan was that I was to be summoned to a meeting with the two of you, having been accused of . . .something.

By...someone.

You would know the details; I would know nothing. Then you would hand me an accusatory letter from the "Black Lives Matter Team" - with no names.

Is this how the UU Good Officer usually handles such matters? How delightfully Kafkaesque.

There is no doubt that some people both of and not-of color were inflamed at the (name event). They expressed their inflammation heatedly, if not coherently.

However, there were other people of color present who were not inflamed. Instead, they afterward expressed chagrin over what they agreed was a needless and destructive display of incivility, aided and abetted by a moderator who pointedly failed to moderate. One young black man has actually volunteered to testify to this effect to you. Would you like to hear from him?

Or shall we keep it cozy: three middle-aged white (people) discussing second-hand black experiences?

By the way two other young men of color from that audience have asked me for information on careers in law enforcement, and one of the other (POC) panelists wants me bring a (person from profession) to present to his youth group - so it seems inflammation was not the only possible response to what I had to say.

Moreover, I have since met with the woman from the (Organization) who organized the event, and who originally invited me to speak about the effects of trauma on law enforcement officers and what can be done to mitigate those effects. She confirms that I did what I was asked to do, and that nothing I said or did was unexpected, insensitive or unkind.

Moreover, she reassured me that I am not the only one to have been subjected to boorish behavior on the part of some - not all - members of the audience, with the same moderator present. During each of the series of (name) panels, representatives of law enforcement were also greeted with belligerent rudeness, presumably by the same people.

So, it would seem that there were people who showed up at the (name of event) prepared . . . simply to indulge themselves in a display of preexisting hostility toward law enforcement, no matter who represented that profession on a given evening or what he or she had to say, then or afterward.

Though I have heard that there was one panelist who got off comparatively lightly. It's possible that he - a police chief - was somehow less inflammatory than a chaplain talking about responding to tragedy in the (State) woods or a (City) police officer talking about her job as a small town (State) cop . . .

I will not be able to come to the meeting on Friday, owing to work emergencies. It appears that someone at (Congregation) knows how to Google, so they will be able to tell you just what those emergencies are.

Either of you may feel free to call me today if you wish to discuss this like normal people. You might want to let your mysterious Black Lives Matter Team know that "dialogue" and "relationship" (not to mention "connection" and "healing") require the minimal courtesy of letting the person you intend to be in dialogue with know who you are.

With disappointment,

Reverend Rev. Rowan

Rupture and Discord

From: Rev. Goodwright
To: Rev. Rowan, Rev. Acosta

Dear Rev. Rowan and Rev. Acosta,

There has clearly been some kind of rupture or discord as a result of the (name) event, with anger and probably misunderstanding on both sides. (Congregation name) has expressed a desire to work it out, starting with a meeting among the ministers. The purpose of the meeting we were to have had a week ago was for dialogue and to open up communication.

A Good Officer is someone willing to be present and to moderate when people are in tension with one another. I am not a judge or jury, nor am I accusing anyone of anything. I have tried to make clear in my communication that I see two sides to the story - presenting, to the best of my ability, what you, Rev. Acosta, initially expressed as your concern, and lifting up that you, Rev. Rowan, were also upset by what happened at the (name) event.

The covenant UUMA members share with each other is important to us, and we regard a Good Officer's invitation to be one where people can try to work out misunderstandings. I understand, Rev. Rowan, that you do not share the covenantal relationship with either Rev. Acosta or me, because you are not a member of the UUMA. And yet, I still extend the invitation to a conversation, because I think it's important. I see my role as Good Officer as not to be limited to members of the UUMA, but to impartially facilitate conversation, whether everyone participating is UUMA-affiliated or not.

Actually, I believe dialogue and communication are increasingly critical in our all-too-polarized world. Too often and too easily in our current culture, we get painted into corners, we get stuck in our narratives, and we abandon the art of civil communication. My hope is that, by meeting, we might be able to address fallout from an evening that left many people upset. I believe it is important for people to work out their differences.

I agree the letter from the BLM team should have been signed with individuals' names. I have spoken to you, Rev. Acosta, about that, and you agreed, too. My understanding is that, when you spoke to your team, they said they would be willing to share their names. Rev. Acosta, would the BLM team re-issue the letter with names attached?

My understanding also, Rev. Rowan, is that the BLM team said they would be willing to meet you face-to-face. From your email, I gather that would be your preference anyway. Given vacation schedules, the earliest such a meeting could happen is September, or any time after that, whenever you may feel ready.

This email is an invitation, nothing more. From the get-go, my hope has been to invite you to a conversation and dialogue with each other.

Thank you,

Rev. Goodwright, Good Officer

Last Email

The following is the last entry in this email thread.

From: Rev. Rowan
To: Rev. Goodwright, Rev. Acosta

Dear Rev. Goodwright and Rev. Acosta,

Thank you so much for this invitation but having discussed the (named event) with the persons who organized and staffed the event, I feel that all my concerns have been heard and addressed by the relevant parties - a group that does not include the Black Lives Matter Team at (Congregation) or any other UU entity.

While I agree that dialogue is becoming generally more difficult, I would suggest on the basis of the evidence that, in this case, at least, the problem in communication does not lie with me. I identified myself openly, spoke honestly and did not attempt to silence or intimidate my interlocutors or encourage others to do so.

If there is discord between us, that is indeed too bad, but I neither caused nor experienced it. As I do not consider the mere possibility that UUs might disagree to be a problem, let alone a crisis, I am unlikely to prove helpful to those who do.

I wish you and your congregations the best in all your endeavors but must turn down your kind invitation. I consider this matter settled and the subject closed.

Peace

Rev. Rowan

13. Accusation and Polarization II

The following is a Facebook post made by Rev. Kate Rohde in February 2021. It is unedited. The situation described in the Facebook post had been ongoing for about three months. She has given the Fifth Principle Project permission to use her real name and include her Facebook post in this chapter.

The Suspension of Rev. Kate Rohde

My UUMA colleagues will have already heard that I have been "cancelled" (suspended from membership) by the UUMA, the professional organization for UU ministers that I have been a member of for more than 40 years, and to which I gave several thousand hours of volunteer time in many leadership capacities for more than two decades.

Although you know I was suspended, they did not tell you why. Usually, it is for something dire like sexual abuse (although most abusers are not suspended) so I want to tell you that is not the case. Unfortunately, they will not tell me either.

Let me tell you what I know.

- I got a phone call out of the blue from a minister telling me I had "done harm" and did I want to get back "in covenant."
- I asked for correspondence and in that correspondence, I asked what rules I was accused of breaking and what the evidence was that I had done so.
- They refused point blank to tell me. That was "not a part of their process."
- Evidently it was also their process to take the accusations as truth and not to allow any input on my part. Did I want to continue the "Process" and getting back into covenant?

- I asked what, exactly, was the process. I used to know it intimately as I headed up a previous generation's process, but that had been completely revised and ministers voted overwhelmingly to give up anything that looked like due process and protected those falsely accused.
- I checked the "new" code but was not enlightened. Asking someone who was supposed to know, he said he didn't know either and he wasn't sure there was a new process. I was one of the first to be prosecuted under the new regime. The UUMA officials would not answer my question about the process as a whole but they hinted that I would never have an opportunity to question the allegations made against me.
- Although I do not know precisely what the accusers said, I do know that there were three of them, making three different complaints but working together to do so. These were not people I have ever met. My sins appear to be in the form of Facebook posts.
- They then demanded that before I go forward, I had to meet a list of demands. This was evidently in service to the idea I had to stop doing the bad things I was doing - a demand that is only supposed to be in egregious cases, but mine, it seems, was deemed an egregious case. I later learned that the list was drawn up by my accusers themselves.
- Most of the list was fine since they were mostly things I had not done and did not wish to do, but two requests were, for me, not acceptable.
  o One involved never speaking or posting any material at all on a specific topic. This, I felt, would give up my right to freedom of the pulpit and I do not feel they have a legal right to ask that.
  o The other involved cutting off all relationships whatsoever with a group of people I had known many years ago. Although I am not in a close relationship with any of those people, I am Facebook friends with several of them and, again, I do not think the UUMA has a right to tell me to unfriend them. I tried to negotiate this

down to something acceptable, but they would not budge.

- I found out the person in charge of the process going forward was a person who has publicly defamed me and is close friends of one of the accusers. She would not recuse herself.

- I wrote a letter saying I found the process unjust and abusive and would subject myself to it no further. Over a month later I received a letter suspending me from membership.

My Next Steps

I am consulting a civil rights attorney locally who thinks I may have a good case. I would drop it, but I think this move of controlling the speech and thoughts of ministers is anathema to UUism and someone has to push back. I am not the first nor will I be the last. My infraction is so small, if it even exists, that anyone could be found guilty given just a little animus of an accuser and stupidity of those in charge of the process.

I invite anyone who cares to write the UUMA or the UUA in opposition to these kinds of increasingly anti-liberal, anti-UU practices. If you would like to help with expenses, message me. I am upset at the demise of an organization that was once important to me and my removal from it, but more upset that Unitarian Universalism at the national level and at some local levels is being replaced by a religious devotion to Critical Theory which puts it above our democratic, liberal, principles.

Authors' Conclusion: The Path to Fear and Polarization

We at the Fifth Principle Project believe our denomination has arrived at a terrible place. A mere accusation now carries with it the assumption of being "guilty as charged." Additionally, there is no hesitation from officially sanctioned UU organizations such as the UUMA to move forward on charges based on undocumented or anonymous sources. Unsigned declarations and opinions masquerading as facts are considered sufficient evidence to commence disciplinary action. If an accused resist or fails to appear before a demanded tribunal, that resistance itself becomes sufficient grounds for further action. Such was the case with Rev. Dr. Eklof. As noted in Chapter 10, "Good Officer Account," we learned that the Ministerial Fellowship Committee noted in its June 2019 letter of dis-fellowship to Rev. Eklof that the decision to remove Rev. Eklof from fellowship "was made based on the Rev. Dr. Eklof's refusal to engage with the fellowship review process . . ."[164]

We saw in Chapter 12, "Accusation and Polarization I" the repercussions that Rev. Rowan may have faced if that minister had been a member of the Unitarian Universalist Ministers' Association. Once confronted by an anonymous accusation and a summons to provide an accounting, simply questioning the charges and showing reluctance to engage until questions are answered can be perceived as an injustice itself. That is, all the clarifying information requested by Rev. Rowan such as documentation of the charge and the request that accusers identify themselves, could have been considered a failure to engage and thus grounds for disciplinary action.

The situation in Chapter 13, "Accusation and Polarization II" is different in that Rev. Kate Rohde, although retired, was and had been a member of the Unitarian Universalist Ministers' Association. Thus, the UUMA could claim some right to intervene. What is striking is the similarity of the actions taken by the UUMA. As with Rev. Rowan and Rev. Rohde, unspecified accusations were received and acted upon by the UUMA. For Rev. Rohde apparently for comments made on Facebook. Repeated requests for information about the substance of the accusation were ignored while demands for changes in behavior were made. All the while, the process for clarifying the charges and the process to adjudicate the accusation remained opaque.

Since there is no accountability for making an accusation, UUism has entered a self-perpetuating cycle where fear of being accused of "something" must be considered every time a minister speaks. This fear of being charged with causing "harm" is not theoretical.

If the authors of this book properly interpreted the UUMA guidelines, a single word change in the draft of the May 2019 UUMA Ethical Standards greatly expanded the jurisdiction of UUMA oversight to personal conversations. In the phrase in the Ethical Standards, "I will not engage in **public words** or actions that degrade the vocation of ministry," the word "public" was removed. What comfort can a minister have that coffee shop conversations are free from official rebuke?

What has become of UUism? As mentioned earlier, many of our congregations have covenants that encourage direct communication, open dialogue, and respectful listening. Rev. Goodwright made an insightful observation:

> Actually, I believe dialogue and communication are increasingly critical in our all-too-polarized world. Too often and too easily in our current culture, we get painted into corners, we get stuck in our narratives, and we abandon the art of civil communication.

To be clear, this is not the UUism that we must accept. Throughout this book, we have provided observations on how our UU leadership is attempting to move UUism to an authoritarian model more characteristic of orthodox religions. If we have the will and the courage to speak, our Fifth Principle will enable UUs to defend and preserve the Unitarian Universalism liberal values and heritage. Speak now or forever be silenced.

Appendix A: Seven Principles

1st Principle: The inherent worth and dignity of every person;

2nd Principle: Justice, equity and compassion in human relations;

3rd Principle: Acceptance of one another and encouragement to spiritual growth in our congregations;

4th Principle: A free and responsible search for truth and meaning;

5th Principle: The right of conscience and the use of the democratic process within our congregations and in society at large;

6th Principle: The goal of world community with peace, liberty, and justice for all;

7th Principle: Respect for the interdependent web of all existence of which we are a part.

Appendix B: Six Sources

- Direct experience of that transcending mystery and wonder, affirmed in all cultures, which moves us to a renewal of the spirit and an openness to the forces which create and uphold life;
- Words and deeds of prophetic people which challenge us to confront powers and structures of evil with justice, compassion, and the transforming power of love;
- Wisdom from the world's religions which inspires us in our ethical and spiritual life;
- Jewish and Christian teachings which call us to respond to God's love by loving our neighbors as ourselves;
- Humanist teachings which counsel us to heed the guidance of reason and the results of science, and warn us against idolatries of the mind and spirit;
- Spiritual teachings of Earth-centered traditions which celebrate the sacred circle of life and instruct us to live in harmony with the rhythms of nature.

Appendix C: Alt-Right Accusation

The insistence that *The Gadfly Papers* is allied with alt-right ideology has, in turn, led to the accusation by some that Rev. Dr. Eklof is himself a closet alt-right UU minister. This charge is found mostly online in Facebook discussions and blogs. One online example of this is found in a blog that is referred to as a resource for Rev. Rothbauer's 2020 General Assembly presentation. It is from Andrew J. Mackay, and it's entitled, "A Unitarian Universalist Pipeline to the Right?" (2019). This is a short essay in a series of four, but this one tells the reader to be very wary of UUs who talk about "postmodernism," "political correctness," "identity politics," or "Critical Race Theory" in a negative way, for they may be sliding toward an embrace of the alt-right. Dr. Eklof criticizes all these ideas, so the implication is clear enough.

Another notable example depicting Dr. Eklof as some kind of alt-righter in liberal clothing is found in a 64-page rebuttal of *The Gadfly Papers* entitled *What the Gadfly Papers Gets Wrong*, penned by one of Eklof's former congregants, Elissa Lowe. She suggests this several times, at one point even comparing Dr. Eklof to Donald Trump. We provide a link to her piece below. But we also provide a link to a rebuttal of her piece, both on the Fifth Principle Project website. https://fifthprincipleproject.org/wp-content/uploads/2020/08/Gadfly_Critique-2.pdf

https://fifthprincipleproject.org/2020/08/08/a-reply-to-elissa-lowe-on-what-the-gadfly-papers-gets-wrong

Appendix D: We Quit

By UU Ministers

To: UUMA Board of Trustees to be delivered and take effect September 15, 2020.

From: Disaffected Colleagues

We write to express our profound disappointment with recent developments in the UUMA and its new norms of thought, behavior, and procedure. We highlight below three of the most relevant events of the past year or so.

Public Letters of Condemnation

Public Letters of Condemnation from groups of colleagues (DRUMM, POCI Chapter, 'White Ministers') in June 2019 denouncing *The Gadfly Papers* and its author, Todd Eklof. Of course, it is okay to criticize published views—we might not be all of one mind about *The Gadfly Papers* ourselves. But these letters of condemnation are a stain upon our collegiality in several respects, the most prominent of which are:

- Making charges of racism, ableism, classism, homophobia, transphobia, vitriolic rhetoric, alt-right ideology, and white supremacy culture without citing any particulars.
- The rejection of reason and logic, calling them expressions of white supremacy.
- The fact that hundreds of colleagues signed one or more of these letters within 24 hours of the book's release—few

could have read it, much less reflected upon it. Plus, the letters (and therefore the colleagues) preemptively reject the idea that it's necessary to read something before publicly condemning it and its author.

- The mob mentality which all this reflects—condemning hurriedly at the urging of others rather than forming one's own view of the matter. It seemed everybody was eager to get in a kick—a disgraceful episode.

The UUMA Board's censure of Todd Eklof

The Board's conduct in issuing censure has been disheartening and relationship-breaking.

- Echoing the other letters of condemnation in disavowing logic, calling it a strategy of white supremacy culture.
- Citing no particulars from the book as evidence of its offense.
- Violating the disciplinary process defined in our UUMA Code of Conduct—not just minor deviation, but dispensing with the most basic rudiments of fairness, like notification of the charges, presentation of evidence, and the opportunity to respond.

Disingenuousness about the basis for censure:

- In order to deflect charges of censorship, claiming the censure was not about the content of the book, although the first sentence of the censure letter states that it was about exactly that.
- Claiming the censure was really about Eklof's "refusal to engage" with his critics and the Board—implausible because that was never mentioned in the censure letter.
- Most preposterous, claiming that the public letter of censure was not a disciplinary action, not a professional admonition,

and not a formal reprimand (and therefore not subject to the procedures required in the Code).

It is heartbreaking to find the leaders of our professional association engaging in such astonishing deception and double-think. Under these standards of dishonesty, how is any genuine relationship possible, much less 'covenant' or 'beloved community'?

When challenged on its behavior, the Board might have said, *"Upon reflection, we were wrong to censure the way we did. We panicked under pressure. We have re-thought the matter and will [a] rescind the illegitimate censure, and [b] pursue a fresh course of action consistent with our rules and our covenantal values."* This could have included a genuine discussion of *Gadfly* and its effects (rather than a uni-directional scold) or even a fresh censure process on a legitimate basis. But in the present state of UUMA culture, that was evidently not a viable avenue for the board. Condemnation must be swift and unquestioning, or one's status as an 'ally' of the oppressed may be in question.

June 2020 Annual Meeting

The most recent and decisive event was the approval by the UUMA membership of an overhaul of our Code of Conduct. The new approach was said to be 'more covenantal,' and yet greatly amped up rules and enforcement. Although some features of the new Code have merit, in several important respects it is deeply disturbing. Some of the new offenses outlined in the Code are outrageous, if not patently absurd.

- It is now Bullying & Emotional Abuse (defined in the Appendix) to exhibit a pattern of:
- "challenging a person's perceptions, opinions, and thoughts"
- "switching topics" or
- "using words or other means to stop a conversation."

This is so absurd as to require no further comment.

The new offense of Tokenism includes: "any superficial gesture" or "sense by a member of the dominant group of fulfilling an ethical mandate, of 'doing the right thing,' or of avoiding criticism" in efforts toward diversity, equity, and inclusion. While superficial gestures can indeed be irksome, it is outrageous—perhaps fanatical—to mandate diversity, equity, and inclusion but then make it misconduct to seem to be doing it to fulfill a mandate.

The language throughout the new Code conveys the implicit presumption of guilt and places the aggrieved colleague almost entirely in control of the process—an apparent rejection of the very notion of fairness.

Perhaps most shocking is the complete elimination of due process in the enforcement of our Code. This is chilling in itself. Further, it is indicative of fanaticism that our colleagues see it as 'covenantal' to discipline or expel a member without even specifying the offending behavior and providing the opportunity to respond to the allegations.

In the amendments debate, 'con' statements seldom even addressed the merits of the amendment in question. Most implied that any criticism of the proposed overhaul, no matter how carefully measured and reasoned, was a kind of oppression, inflicting fresh trauma upon marginalized colleagues.

This whole dispiriting episode dispelled for us any remaining doubt that our professional association has become entranced with an illiberal, even anti-liberal, ideology.

Conclusion

Numerous letters have been sent by colleagues to the board expressing alarm at the growing dogmatism and intolerance in our UUMA. A group from Return to a Democratic Faith met with board representatives in April 2020 for a detailed discussion of the board's conduct in issuing censure, and its implications. The discussion was civil but produced no genuine engagement with the concerns raised. Amendments were proposed to mitigate the worst aspects of the Code overhaul in June 2020, which were not only rejected by 85-90% of the membership but unfairly characterized as hostile.

It is apparent the UUMA leadership, and a large majority of members, now reject the Enlightenment values which have always been baseline conditions of our faith and have inspired social progress for several centuries. These values have been replaced by a vision of cultural revolution guided by identity politics and White Supremacy Culture jargon. Ritual confession of identity-based guilt and virtue-signaling are now primary practices. We may be supportive of many of the anti-oppressive *aspirations* of this movement but find the dogmatism and the unreflective revolutionary fervor repugnant and destructive.

Despite (for many of us) long years of cherished ministerial collegiality, the UUMA has become for us an inhospitable place and an embarrassment. As it has been made clear that genuine dialog on the new orthodoxy will not be tolerated in our ministerial association, we cannot in good faith continue our association with it.

And so, with great sorrow, we withdraw our membership from the UUMA.

Footnotes

History

White Supremacy: How the Decision was Made

[1] Elaine McArdle, "Critics See White Supremacy in UUA Hiring Practices," *UU World Magazine,* March 27, 2017, https://www.uuworld.org/articles/critics-challenge-uua-hiring-practices.

[2] McArdle, "Critics See White Supremacy." In an email, Tayler told *UU World Magazine* that the UUA has "an affirmative action policy through which fully qualified minority status candidates are given preference over fully qualified non-minority candidates. I can also share that I have followed that policy in all of my hires. So while I can't speak about Christina's interview process directly, I can say that if Christina had been one of the final candidates and if I had considered her fully qualified, I would have offered her the job."

[3] McArdle, "Critics See White Supremacy."

[4] Rev. Peter Morales, Facebook, May 7, 2017. The Facebook posts reads in part, "The two topics which compel me to speak are the acceptance and repetition of a false narrative and, as a result of that narrative, the terrible way a number of colleagues have been treated . . . The narrative is that she [Christina Rivera] was not hired because she is a Latina. Let me be as clear as I can be: this is simply false . . . The uncritical acceptance of a false narrative and the assumption of moral inferiority of leaders led naturally to what looks more like an inquisition than like the Beloved Community. This is my second point: the Beloved Community does not throw people under the bus."

[5] UUA Board of Trustees Videoconference Meeting Minutes, "UUA Interim Presidency Transition Plan," April 3, 2017, https://www.uua.org/files/pdf/i/interim_pres_plan_04042017.pdf.

[6] UUA Board of Trustees Videoconference Meeting Minutes, "Motion to Endorse UU White Supremacy Teach In," April 3, 2017, https://www.uua.org/sites/live-new.uua.org/files/wh_sup_tchin_motn_04032017.pdf.

Fifth Principle Task Force Report

[7] UUA Board of Trustees Videoconference Meeting Minutes, January 21-23, 2021. https://www.uua.org/files/2021-01/full_packet_01212021.pdf.

[8] Donald E. Skinner, "Big Changes Proposed for UUA's General Assembly," *UU World*, January 15, 2010, https://www.uuworld.org/articles/changes-ga.

[9] Davidoff served as the chairperson for the Fifth Principle Task Force from January 2008 to October 2009. Afterward Joe Sullivan served as the chair from October 2009 to December 2009, https://www.uua.org/files/documents/boardtrustees/5thprinciple/0912_report.pdf.

[10] "Unitarian Universalist Association Bylaws and Rules, Article II Principles and Purposes," Section C-2.2. Purposes, as amended through October 18, 2019, https://www.uua.org/files/pdf/u/uua_bylaws_2019.pdf.

[11] "UUA Fifth Principle Task Force, Reformulating our General Assembly: Status Quo is Not an Option," https://www.uua.org/files/documents/boardtrustees/5thprinciple/0906_presentation.pdf.

[12] "Fifth Principle Task Force Report to the UUA Board of Trustees," Unitarian Universalist Association, December 2009, 2-3, https://www.uua.org/files/documents/boardtrustees/5thprinciple/0912_report.pdf.

[13] "Fifth Principe Task Force Report," 3-4.

[14] "Fifth Principe Task Force Report," 11.

[15] "Fifth Principe Task Force Report," 4. The report further commented, "We believe our recommendations lay out a vision for effective governance that reflect core values of our liberal faith and the imperative for bringing the leadership of member congregations and our Association together in mutually accountable relationship around matters of greatest importance to the present and future vitality of our UU movement."

[16] Jane Greer, "UUA Board Considers Far-Reaching Governance Reform." *UU World*, January 25, 2010, https://www.uuworld.org/articles/governance-

reform. Other governance actions considered by the board were changes to the term of office for the president and moderator, the composition of the presidential search committee and a process to nominate officers by petition.

[17] Michelle Bates Deakin, "Board Finalizes Bylaws for Vote at General Assembly." *UU World*, April 25, 2011, https://www.uuworld.org/articles/bylaw-vote-ga-2011.

[18] Letter from the UUA Board of Trustees to public, "Transforming Governance for the Second Half-Century," found in the Agenda for the Special Meeting of the UUA Board of Trustees, February 4, 2010, 1, 2010, https://www.uua.org/files/documents/boardtrustees/100204_agenda.pdf.

[19] "Transforming Governance for the Second Half-Century," 2-3.

[20] "Transforming Governance for the Second Half-Century," 4.

[21] "Fiftieth General Assembly of the Unitarian Universalist Association, held in Charlotte, North Carolina," June 2011, https://www.harvardsquarelibrary.org/wp-content/uploads/2019/09/GA-Minutes-2011.pdf. The vote impacted the following sections of the Bylaws: 6.3, 6.4, 6.5, 6.6, 6.8, 8.3, 8.7, 9.1, 9.3, 9.4, 9.6, 9.11, 9.12, 9.13 and Rule G-9.12.2. Note: The meeting minutes incorrectly list the date of the assembly as June 22, 2010. The correct year is 2011.

[22] Jane Greer, "Board focused on planning for 2012 General Assembly," *UU World*, February 7, 2011, https://www.uuworld.org/articles/board-plans-2012-ga.

[23] Greer, "Board focused on planning for 2012 General Assembly."

[24] "Toward an Anti-Racist Unitarian Universalist Association," 1997 Business Resolution, https://www.uua.org/action/statements/toward-anti-racist-unitarian-universalist-association.

[25] "Strategic Review of Professional Ministries," Unitarian Universalist Association, March 2011, https://www.uua.org/files/documents/mpl/110406_srpm.pdf. The report noted earlier efforts to advance multiculturalism and anti-racism. Most notably was the Black Empowerment Movement of the 1960s and 1970s that sought to engage UUism in a kind of restorative justice toward the African American community. Conflicts over strategies between the Black Affairs

Council (BAC) and the Black and White Alliance (an integrated group called BAWA) and the Association's failure to fulfill its financial commitment to supporting Black empowerment resulted in an estimated 1,500 African American UUs and white allies leaving the Association. In the 1980s the board commissioned the Institutional Racial Audit Report and the appointment of a Racism Monitoring and Assessment Team. The General Assembly in 1985 overcame opposition to establish a Black Concerns Working Group to implement recommendations of the Task Force on Racism. The Committee on Urban Concerns in Ministry focused on issues of oppression and racism in urban areas. The focus on "urban ministry" was instrumental in the founding of the African American UU Ministers (AAUUM). However, it wasn't until the 1990s that the Association made more intensive efforts to transform Unitarian Universalism through programs that addressed antiracism, anti-oppression, and multiculturalism. Several identity-based groups evolved during this period, including the Latino/a Unitarian Universalist Networking Alliance (LUUNA), and, through the negotiations between LUUNA and AAUUM, the people of color organization known today as Diverse and Revolutionary Unitarian Universalist Multicultural Ministries (DRUUMM).

[26] "Call for Reflection on the Fifth Principle Task Force Report," Unitarian Universalist Association, January 24, 2020, https://www.uua.org/uuagovernance/committees/cic/blog/call-reflection-fifth-principle-task.

COIC: Widening the Circle of Concern

[27] Zack Beauchamp, "The Controversy Around Hoax Studies in Critical Theory, Explained," *Vox*, October 15, 2018, https://www.vox.com/2018/10/15/17951492/grievance-studies-sokal-squared-hoax. The academics involved were Helen Pluckrose, a magazine editor, James Lindsay, a mathematician and Peter Boghossian, a philosopher. Also see, Tristin Hopper, "'Dog Park are Petri Dishes for Cannie Rape Culture,' and more Ridiculous Studies Hoaxsters got Published in Academic Journals," National Post, October 4, 2018, https://nationalpost.com/news/world/dog-parks-are-petri-dishes-for-canine-rape-culture-and-more-of-the-ridiculous-studies-a-team-of-hoaxsters-got-published-in-academic-journals.

[28] "Theology," in *Widening the Circle of Concern, Report of the UUA Commission on Institutional Change*, (Boston, MA, Unitarian Universalist Association, 2020), 12.

[29] "Theology," in *Widening the Circle of Concern*, 9.

[30] Unitarian Universalist Ministers' Association (UUMA) Board of Trustees and Executive Team, "UUMA Elected Board of Trustees and Executive Team Issues Public Letter of Censure, August 17, 2019, https://www.uuma.org/news/466020/UUMA-Board-and-Executive-Team-Issues-Public-Letter-of-Censure.htm.

[31] "Methodology," in *Widening the Circle of Concern*, "Call for Testimony," xxi.

[32] "Methodology," in *Widening the Circle of Concern*, "Call for Testimony," xxi.

[33] Sybille Krämer, Sigrid Weigel, "Testimony/Bearing Witness: Epistemology, Ethics, History and Culture", (Rowman & Littlefield, August 23, 2017), 146.

Martin Kusch, "Analysing holocaust survivor testimony. Certainties, Scepticism, Relativism," This is the penultimate draft of a paper to be published by Rowman & Littlefield, in a volume on testimony to be edited by Sybille Krämer, 14, https://emergenceofrelativism.weebly.com/uploads/7/6/7/1/76714317/kusch.h olocaust.testimony.pdf.

[34] "Methodology," in *Widening the Circle of Concern*, "Call for Personal Testimony," xxiv.

[35] "Methodology," in *Widening the Circle of Concern*, xxv.

[36] "Methodology," in *Widening the Circle of Concern*, "Confidentiality of Data," xxii.

[37] An eighth principle has been proposed to be included in the UUA's current Seven Principles. The proposed principle reads, "We, the member congregations of the Unitarian Universalist Association, covenant to affirm and promote: journeying toward spiritual wholeness by working to build a diverse multicultural Beloved Community by our actions that accountably dismantle racism and other oppressions in ourselves and our institutions." See https://www.8thprincipleuu.org.

[38] "Governance," in *Widening the Circle of Concern,* "Lay Leader of Color Avatar," 38.

[39] "Innovations and Risk Taking," in *Widening the Circle of Concern,* "White Counter Narrative Avatar," 109.

[40] "Trends," in *Widening the Circle of Concern,* 1-5.

[41] "Trends," in *Widening the Circle of Concern,* 2.

[42] "Preface," in *Widening the Circle of Concern,* ix.

[43] "Preface," in *Widening the Circle of Concern,* ix.

[44] "Methodology," in *Widening the Circle of Concern,* xxv.

[45] "Strategic Review of Professional Ministries. An exploration of the past, present, challenges and opportunities for our Unitarian Universalist ministries, with sixty recommendations to consider," (Boston: MA, Unitarian Universalist Association of Congregations, March 2011), 3-6, https://www.uua.org/files/documents/mpl/110406_srpm.pdf.

[46] "Unitarian Universalist Demographics from ARIS and FACT Surveys," accessed from "Demographic and Statistical Information about Unitarian Universalism," https://www.uua.org/data/demographics.

[47] "America's Changing Religious Landscape," Pew Research Center's Religion & Public Life Project, May 12, 2015, https://www.pewforum.org/2015/05/12/americas-changing-religious-landscape/.

[48] Caryle Murphy, "The Most and Least Educated U.S. Religious Groups," Pew Research Center, November 4, 2016, https://www.pewresearch.org/fact-tank/2016/11/04/the-most-and-least-educated-u-s-religious-groups/.

[49] "Why America's 'Nones' Don't Identify with a Religion," Pew Research Center, August 8, 2018, https://www.pewresearch.org/fact-tank/2018/08/08/why-americas-nones-dont-identify-with-a-religion/.

COIC Scope and Implications

[50] Board of Trustees, Unitarian Universalist Association, Meeting Minutes, January 24-25, 2020, Boston, MA, https://www.uua.org/files/2020-09/bot_min_01242020.pdf.

[51] "Article II Study Commission," https://www.uua.org/uuagovernance/committees/article-ii-study-commission.

[52] Board of Trustees, Unitarian Universalist Association, Meeting Minutes, September 14, 2020, Zoom Teleconference, https://www.uua.org/files/2020-10/bot_min_09142020.pdf.

[53] DRUUM – Diverse Revolutionary Unitarian Universalist Ministers, TRUUst – Transgender Religious professional Unitarian Universalists Together, and EqUUal Access – organization focused on providing equal access to UUs with disabilities.

[54] "Appendix II - Theology," in *Widening the Circle of Concern, Report of the UUA Commission on Institutional Change, (Boston, MA, Unitarian Universalist Association, 2020)*, 172.

[55] "Appendix II - Theology," in *Widening the Circle of Concern*, 178.

[56] "Governance" in *Widening the Circle of Concern*, 22.

[57] "Methodology," in *Widening the Circle of Concern*, "Confidentiality of Data," xxii.

[58] "Governance" in *Widening the Circle of Concern*, "Recommendations about UUA Bylaws, from Visions, Inc.," 22.

[59] "Constitution and By-laws, Article II, Section 4," Unitarian Universalist Association, Directory 1961 - 1962, p 25, (seq 31), Boston: Unitarian Universalist Association of Congregations, [1961]-2009, Andover-Harvard Theological Library, Harvard University, https://nrs.harvard.edu/urn-3:DIV.LIB:30758222?n=31.

[60] Conrad Wright, "A Doctrine of Church of Liberals," in *Walking Together: Polity and Participation in Unitarian Universalist Churches* (Boston, MA: Unitarian Universalist Association, 1989), 4.

[61] "Governance," in *Widening the Circle of Concern,* 26.

[62] "Unitarian Universalist Tradition: A Short History," Unitarian Universalist Association, https://www.uua.org/leadership/learning-center/governance/polity/47003.shtml. See footnote 5: After the Cambridge Platform of 1648 came the Half Way Covenant of 1657, the Savoy Declaration of 1658, the "Reforming Synod" of 1679, the "Heads of Agreement" of 1691, the Proposals of 1705, and the Saybrook Platform of 1708. Another four documents followed by 1883. This webpage and the information provided on it is part of the Unitarian Universalist Association LeaderLab program. LeaderLab fulfills the mission statements presented by President Rev. Susan Frederick-Gray to "equip congregations, train and credential leaders and advance UU values."

[63] "Governance" in *Widening the Circle of Concern,* 27.

[64] Conrad Wright, "Unitarian Universalist Denominational Structure," in *Walking Together: Polity and Participation in Unitarian Universalist Churches* (Boston, MA: Unitarian Universalist Association, 1989), 74.

[65] "Theological Perspective," in *Interdependence: Renewing Congregational Polity,* https://www.uua.org/leadership/learning-center/governance/polity/47002.shtml.

[66] "Fifth Principle Task Force Report to the UUA Board of Trustees," Unitarian Universalist Association, December 2009, 2, https://www.uua.org/files/documents/boardtrustees/5thprinciple/0912_report.pdf.

[67] Unitarian Universalist Board of Trustees, "Choosing Committee Assignments," October 15, 2020, https://www.uua.org/files/2020-10/full_packet_10132020.pdf. On page 3 of the "UUA Board of Trustees, Orientation to Board Culture and Decision-Making October 15, 2020," there is a reference to the board's "Accountability Entity – to Our Sources of Accountability and Authority." Those sources are later defined in the "Choosing Committee Assignments" document on an unnumbered page with the heading of Sources. "The Board of Trustees governs on behalf of and is accountable to our Sources of Authority and Accountability ('Sources'), which we have defined as: Our member congregations, Current and future generations of Unitarian Universalists, The heritage, traditions, and ideals of

Unitarian Universalism, The vision of Beloved Community, The Spirit of life, love, and the holy."

[68] "Preface," in *Widening the Circle of Concern*, vii.

[69] "Theology" in *Widening the Circle of Concern*, "Centering Theology: A Conversation About Faith, Race, Liberalism, Part 4," 13.

[70] "Living Our Values in the World," in *Widening the Circle of Concern*, 72.

[71] "Innovations and Risk-Taking," in *Widening the Circle of Concern*, 105.

[72] "Methodology," in *Widening the Circle of Concern*, xxiii.

[73] "Governance," in *Widening the Circle of Concern*, "Restructuring the Moderator and President Positions, by the Commission on Governance," 24. The recommendation in *Widening the Circle of Concern* is taken from the April 24, 1993 report "The Commission on Governance Recommendations."

[74] Letter from Rev. Don Southworth to UUA Board of Trustees, April 16, 2017, https://cdn.ymaws.com/www.uuma.org/resource/resmgr/docs/DS_Public_Letter_to_Board.pdf.

[75] "Elected Officers of the Unitarian Universalist Association," Unitarian Universalist Association, https://www.uua.org/uuagovernance/officers.

[76] Jessica York, Carey McDonald, Janice Marie Johnson, "Commission on Institutional Change's final report is a critical waypoint, not the end of the journey," *UU World*, Fall 2020, 55-56. Note: Jessica York is the Director of Congregational Life, Carey McDonald is the Executive Vice-president of the UUA and Janice Marie Johnson is the co-director of Ministries and Faith Development.

Article II Study Commission: Story of our Principles

[77] "Article II Study Commission," https://www.uua.org/uuagovernance/committees/article-ii-study-commission. Note: The contents of this URL have changed.

[78] "Article II Study Commission"

[79] "Theology," in *Widening the Circle of Concern, Report of the UUA Commission on Institutional Change*," (Boston: Unitarian Universalist

Association, 2020), 7. This quote is from an address Rev. Dr. Sofia Betancourt delivered at the Service of the Living Tradition in 2018.

[80] "Trends," in *Widening the Circle of Concern*, 5.

[81] "Theology," in *Widening the Circle of Concern*, 16. The term "equitable future" carries two meanings. People can interpret equitable to mean fair or an ideal state of being just and impartial. However, in context of the COIC report, "This will lay the groundwork for our work around truth, transformation and reparations," the term "equitable" could be interpreted as the need for a reparation for past acts so that everyone could be considered as having started from the same place.

[82] "Destructive Behavior Policies," Unitarian Universalist Association, https://www.uua.org/safe/destructive-behavior-policies.

[83] "Constitution and By-Laws, Constitution," 1961, Article II, Section 2, p 24 (seq. 3), Unitarian Universalist Association, Directory. Boston: Unitarian Universalist Association of Congregations, [1961]-2009, Andover-Harvard Theological Library, Harvard University, https://nrs.harvard.edu/urn-3:DIV.LIB:30758222?n=30.

[84] Russell E. Miller, "And Flow on Together: Unitarian-Universalist Consolidation, 1937-1961," in *The Larger Hope, The Second Century of the Universalist Church in America, 1870-1970*, (Boston, MA: Unitarian Universalist Association, 1985), 659. Miller's original footnote reads, "Three reports were made by the Commission at the Syracuse meeting. It was the 'Third Syracuse Report,' including all amendments, that was finally adopted."

[85] "Amendments to the Constitution," *The Monthly Journal of the American Unitarian Association*, 9:5, June 1868, 286, https://books.google.com/books?id=51Y2AAAAMAAJ&newbks=1&newbks_red ir=0&dq=%22bylaws%22%20of%20%22American%20Unitarian%20Associatio n%22&pg=PA286#v=onepage&q=%22bylaws%22%20&f=false.

[86] "By-laws of the American Unitarian Association, as Revised and Adopted at the Annual Meeting, May 23, 1951, p 13, (seq. 15), Unitarian Universalist Association. *Unitarian Year Book September 1, 1951 – August 31, 1952 and Annual Report for 1950 – 1951*, Andover-Harvard Theological Library, Harvard University, https://nrs.harvard.edu/urn-3:DIV.LIB:32542353?n=15.

[87] Russell E, Miller, "Establishing a Theological Base," in *The Larger Hope* (Boston, MA: Unitarian Universalist Association, 1979), 45-47.

[88] "Universalist General Convention, Minutes, Boston: The Convention 1935," October 23-25, 1935, p 3, (seq 3), Unitarian Universalist Association, Directory. Boston: Unitarian Universalist Association of Congregations, [1961]-2009, Andover-Harvard Theological Library, Harvard University, https://nrs.harvard.edu/urn-3:DIV.LIB:33682357?n=3. The Universalist Convention was held in Washington, D.C.

[89] "First General Assembly of Unitarian Universalist Association," May 24, 1962, p 237, (seq. 247), Unitarian Universalist Association. Directory. Boston: Unitarian Universalist Association of Congregations, [1961]-2009, Andover-Harvard Theological Library, Harvard University, https://nrs.harvard.edu/urn-3:DIV.LIB:30758460?n=247.

[90] "Second General Assembly of Unitarian Universalist Association," 1963, 58 (seq. 64), 1964, Unitarian Universalist Association. Directory. Boston: Unitarian Universalist Association of Congregations, [1961]-2009, Andover-Harvard Theological Library, Harvard University, https://nrs.harvard.edu/urn-3:DIV.LIB:30758764?n=64.

[91] "Second General Assembly of Unitarian Universalist Association," p 62 (seq 68), Unitarian Universalist Association. Directory. Boston: Unitarian Universalist Association of Congregations, [1961]-2009, Andover-Harvard Theological Library, Harvard University, https://nrs.harvard.edu/urn-3:DIV.LIB:30758764?n=68.

[92] Donald E. Skinner, "Time to Review the Principles," *UUA World*, April 21, 2006, https://www.uuworld.org/articles/reexamination-uua-principles-announced.

[93] "Unitarian Universalist Association Bylaws and Rules," Article XV, C-15.1, c, 6, "If no study process of Article II has occurred for a period of fifteen years, the Board of Trustees shall appoint a commission to study Article II for not more than two years and to recommend appropriate revisions, if any, thereto to the Board of Trustees for inclusion on the agenda of the next regular General Assembly."

94 "Report of the Unitarian Universalist Commission on Appraisal, On the Mandated Review of Article II of the UUA Bylaws," December 19, 2008, 6, https://www.uua.org/files/documents/coa/081219_boardreport.pdf.

95 Peter Hughes, "Beloved Quotes Produced by the UU Rumor Mill," *UU World*, September 17, 2012, https://www.uuworld.org/articles/uu-rumor-mill-produces-quotes. The quote "Give them, not hell, but hope and courage" first appeared in a pamphlet published in 1951.

96 "UUA Membership Statistics, 1961-2020," Unitarian Universalist Association, https://www.uua.org/data/demographics/uua-statistics. Demographic and Statistical Information about Unitarian Universalism.

97 Christopher L. Walton, "General Assembly Narrowly Rejects New 'Principles and Purposes'," *UU World, July* 6, 2009, https://www.uuworld.org/articles/ga-rejects-new-principles-purposes.

98 Doug Muder, "Confessions of a Virgin Delegate," blog, June 28, 2009, http://ga2009.blogs.uua.org/2009/06/28/confessions-of-a-virgin-delegate/.

99 "Welcome, Inclusion, Affirmation, and Non-discrimination Statements," Washington Ethical Society, Washington, DC., https://www.uua.org/lgbtq/welcoming/ways/welcome-statements.

100 "Responsive Resolution on Inclusions," Minutes, Forty-eighth General Assembly of the Unitarian Universalist Association Held in Salt Lake City, June 24, 2009, 6, https://www.harvardsquarelibrary.org/wp-content/uploads/2019/09/GA-Minutes-2009.pdf.

What a Difference One Year Makes

101 Melissa Harris-Petty, "Who Are We, Our Open and Collective Work," *UU World*, Seeker #1 (2016), 4.

102 Harris-Petty, "Who Are We, Our Open and Collective Work."

103 Galen Guengerich, "What We Believe, Ten Things I Wish People Knew About Unitarian Universalism," *UU World*, Seeker #1 (2016), 10.

104 Christopher L. Walton, "Meet the 'Love People'," *UU World*, Seeker #1 (2016), 22-24.

Theology

New UU Orthodoxy

[105] "COIC: Widening the Circle of Concern," in *Used to Be UU*.

[106] Helen Pluckrose and James Lindsay, "Postmodernism," in *Cynical Theories: How Activist Scholarship Made Everything about Race, Gender, and Identity- and Why This Harms Everybody* (Durham, NC: Pitchstone Publishing, 2020).

[107] *"Cynical Theories,"* Postmodernism's Applied Turn.

[108] Philip E. Devine, *"Human Diversity and the Culture Wars,"* Praeger Publishers, 1996, 29.

[109] *"Human Diversity and the Culture Wars,"* 31.

[110] Stanley J. Grenz, *A Primer on Postmodernism*, Wm B. Eerdman's Publishing 1996, 7.

[111] *"Cynical Theories,"* 41.

[112] *"Human Diversity and the Culture Wars,"* 31.

[113] *"Human Diversity and the Culture Wars,"* 33.

[114] The phrase "post-truth" may not be familiar to most readers. But we all have experienced its consequences in the daily gaslighting effects of "alternative facts" and "fake news" that follow from the impact of the notion that science and reason are merely other forms of discourse, other narratives, other ways of talking about things. Search in Amazon Books for "post truth" or "post-truth" and you will discover a cottage industry of scholars struggling to understand this, its sources, and consequences. All of them find the origins of this era of post-truth in which we are living within postmodernism. And all of them warn the rest of us that we are living in an era in which most of us no longer know who or what to believe, and that this is doing more to undermine faith in our institutions than we are likely able to fathom. For one excellent example see Post-Truth, by Lee McIntyre, The Mit Press, 2018.

[115] *Cynical Theories*, 57-59.

[116] *Cynical Theories*, 48.

[117] *Cynical Theories*, 49-59.

[118] "The Rise and Whys of Grievance Studies," Prof. Helen Pluckrose, Editor in Chief, *Areo Magazine*, Ramsay Center Lectures 2019.

[119] "Innovations and Risk-Taking," in *Widening the Circle of Concern*, 102.

[120] "Governance," in *Widening the Circle of Concern*, 22.

[121] *Cynical Theories*," 48-49.

[122] James Lindsay is a mathematician with a background in physics and is co-founder of New Discourses (newdiscources.com). His books include *Everybody is Wrong about God* and *How to Have Impossible Conversations*. His essays have appeared in numerous outlets, including the Wall Street Journal, Los Angeles Times, and Time.

[123] *Cynical Theories*," 76.

[124] *"Cynical Theories,"* 111.

[125] Crystal M. Fleming, "Why Are We Talking About White Supremacy?" *UU World*, Winter 2018, https://www.uuworld.org/articles/idiots-guide-critical-race-theory.

[126] Khiara M. Bridges, *Critical Race Theory, A Primer*, Foundation Press, 2019 21.

[127] *Critical Race Theory, A Primer*, 21.

[128] *Critical Race Theory, A Primer*, 28.

[129] *Cynical Theories*, 124.

[130] Richard Delgado and Jean Stefancic, *Critical Race Theory, An Introduction*, Dev Publishers, 2017, 3.

[131] AIW (Action of Immediate Witness), "Address 400 Years of White Supremacist Colonialism," adopted at UU General Assembly 2020.

[132] Dr. Elias Ortega, Facebook, June 25, 2020. https://www.facebook.com/Dr.EliasOrtega/posts/10158167584968819

[133] Ortega, Facebook post.

[134] Philip E. Devine, *Human Diversity and the Culture Wars*, 1996; Lukianoff and Haidt, *The Coddling of the American Mind*, 2018; Anne Schneider, *A Self-Confessed White Supremacy Culture*, 2019; Pluckrose and Lindsay, *Cynical Theories*, 2020.

[135] Copyright page in *Widening the Circle of Concern*.

[136] *Engaging Our Theological Diversity*, The Commission on Appraisal of the Unitarian Universalist Association, 2005, 95.

[137] *Engaging Our Theological Diversity*, 84.

[138] *Engaging Our Theological Diversity*, 85.

[139] "The Rise and Whys of Grievance Studies," *Areo Magazine*.

[140] *Engaging Our Theological Diversity*, 97.

[141] John McWorter, "The Dehumanizing Condescension of White Fragility," Atlantic, July 2020; Anne Schneider, *A Self-Confessed White Supremacy Culture, Emergence of an Illiberal Left in Unitarian Universalism*, 2019.

[142] "Acknowledgements," in *Widening the Circle of Concern*, 17.

The Demolition of the Fourth Principle

[143] "The Rise and Whys of Grievance Studies," Prof. Helen Pluckrose, Editor in Chief, *Areo Magazine*, Ramsay Center Lectures 2019, https://www.ramsaycentre.org/wp-content/uploads/2020/06/Pluckrose-Transcript.pdf.

[144] Letter from UUMA Board and Executive Team to Rev. Dr. Todd Eklof, "Issues Public Letter of Censure," August 16, 2019, https://www.uuma.org/news/466020/UUMA-Board-and-Executive-Team-Issues-Public-Letter-of-Censure.htm.

[145] Letter from UU White Ministers to public, "An Open Letter from White UU Ministers," June 23, 2019, https://www.muusja.org/reprint-an-open-letter-from-white-uu-ministers.

[146] "An Open Letter from ARE, Allies for Racial Equity", https://www.facebook.com/notes/allies-for-racial-equity/to-preserve-our-

faith-we-must-do-better-an-invitation-to-white-unitarian-univers/2825278037488426/.

[147] Letter from UU White Ministers to public, "An Open Letter from White UU Ministers," June 23, 2019, https://www.muusja.org/reprint-an-open-letter-from-white-uu-ministers.

[148] Todd F. Eklof, "The Religion of Humanity," in *The Gadfly Papers, Three Inconvenient Essays by One Pesky Minister* (Independently Published, Spokane WA 2019).

[149] Mel Harkrader Pike, "From a Pesky Former UU," blog, July 12, 2019, https://trulyopenmindsandhearts.blog/2019/07/12/from-a-pesky-former-uu/.

[150] "Bylaws and Rules as amended through October 18, 2019," Article II Principles and Purposes, Section C-2.2. Purposes, Unitarian Universalist Association.

[151] "Bylaws and Rules as amended through October 18, 2019," Article XV Amendment, Section 15.2. Submission of Proposed Amendments, Unitarian Universalist Association.

[152] "Bylaws and Rules as amended through October 18, 2019," Article IV General Assembly, Section 4.11. Tentative Agenda for Regular General Assemblies, Unitarian Universalist Association.

[153] The Church of the Larger Fellowship is a Unitarian Universalist Association congregation without walls connecting people all over the world for spiritual growth, worship, learning, and mutual support, https://www.uua.org/beliefs/get-involved/where/clf.

[154] "Voting in UUA Elections," Unitarian Universalist Association, https://www.uua.org/uuagovernance/elections/absentee-voting.

[155] "Bylaws and Rules as amended through October 18, 2019," Article IV General Assembly, Section 4.8 Delegates, (b), Unitarian Universalist Association.

Good Officer

[156] Letter from UUMA People of Color and Indigenous UUMA Chapter to Unitarian Universalist Clergy, "Public Statement," June 22, 2019. The

concluding paragraph of the letter includes, "We call on our white colleagues to resist confusion and renew their dedication to the work of decentering white supremacy. We call on the UUMA to distinguish vitriol and destructive rhetoric from alternative constructive perspectives and, likewise, to enforce the UUMA guidelines."

[157] Letter from UU White Ministers to public, "An Open Letter from White UU Ministers," June 23, 2019, https://www.muusja.org/reprint-an-open-letter-from-white-uu-ministers. The full sentence quoted herein reads, "We recognize that a zealous commitment to 'logic' and 'reason' over all other forms of knowing is one of the foundational stones of White Supremacy Culture."

[158] Letter from UUMA Board and Executive Team to Rev. Dr. Todd Eklof, "Issues Public Letter of Censure," August 16, 2019, https://www.uuma.org/news/466020/UUMA-Board-and-Executive-Team-Issues-Public-Letter-of-Censure.htm. The letter of censure acknowledges that Rev. Eklof was seeking a debate about the direction of UUism but indicates that debate could not be conducted using logic. "We understand from your book that you want **to encourage robust and reasoned debate** about the direction of our faith. However, we cannot ignore the fact that **logic has often been employed in white supremacy culture to stifle dissent**, minimize expressions of harm, and to require those who suffer to prove the harm by that culture's standards." (bold added).

[159] Letter from UUMA Board and Executive Team to Rev. Dr. Todd Eklof, "Issues Public Letter of Censure," August 16, 2019, The Ministerial Fellowship Committee's letter of dis-fellowship was issued on June 8, 2020.

[160] See in this book chapters "COIC: Scope and Implications" and "Article II Study Commission."

[161] Letter from Ministerial Fellowship Committee to Rev. Dr. Eklof, June 8, 2020. The letter reads in part, "The decision was made based on the Rev. Dr. Eklof's refusal to engage with the fellowship review process after a complaint of ethical misconduct was filed by the Liberal Religious Educators Association (LREDA) in January of this year." The letter also alleged that, "They regret that the Rev. Dr. Eklof refused earlier attempts to 'come to the table' after the distribution of his book *The Gadfly Papers* at the UUA General Assembly in Spokane in 2019 was received as harmful... Public contemporary accounts

regarding Rev. Dr. Eklof's engagement level with UUA officials, however, differ from the accounts portrayed in the MFC's letter.

UUMA Board to Ministers: Shut Up

[162] Mel Harkrader Pine, "The UU Crisis, Explained," Truly Open Minds and Hearts, October 17, 2019, https://trulyopenmindsandhearts.blog/2019/10/01/the-uu-crisis-explained/.

[163] Dan Subotnik, "What's Wrong with Critical Race Theory?: Reopening the Case for Middle Class Values: Semantic Scholar," undefined, January 1, 1998, https://digitalcommons.tourolaw.edu/cgi/viewcontent.cgi?article=1186&context=scholarlyworks&httpsredir=1&referer=.

[164] Letter from Ministerial Fellowship Committee to Rev. Dr. Eklof, June 8, 2020.

Made in the USA
Coppell, TX
04 May 2021

54955881R00154